Teaching Post-16 Psychology

Matt Jarvis

.™Nelson Thornes
a Wolters Kluwer business

Published in 2006 by:
Nelson Thornes Ltd
Delta Place
27 Bath Road
CHELTENHAM
GL53 7TH
United Kingdom

06 07 08 09 10 / 10 9 8 7 6 5 4 3 2 1

A catalogue record for this book is available from the British Library

ISBN 0 7487 9418 2

Page make-up by Florence Production Ltd

Printed and bound in Spain by GraphyCems

Contents

Foreword

This book is the first of its kind, as far as I am aware, to take a holistic approach to the teaching of psychology. There is an interesting balance between the more philosophical questions, such as why we should teach psychology in the first place and how it can enhance the wider skills of our young people, and the very practical advice a teacher may need when deciding which to teach, how to teach and what resources to use with whom. Any teacher with responsibility for his or her curriculum area will find the contents of Chapter 2 very helpful indeed when facing the rigours of inspection! I have to admit to getting very excited about how I will be able to use some of the data Matt presents in comparing results between specifications, between schools and colleges, and between subjects.

The pedagogical sections of the book are interesting and helpful in explaining how learning may take place differently in different people, and Matt challenges us to consider how we can apply psychological theory in our teaching. The sections on differentiation and use of information and learning technology (ILT) are particularly helpful to teachers who may have developed a fair range of teaching styles and who may be quite experienced but need to get to grips with the recent advances in ILT and the emphasis being placed on equality and diversity issues. With widening participation in post-16 education in general – and the annual increase of 20% in psychology in particular – we all have a great deal to learn.

My overall opinion of this book is that it is an essential item for the toolkit of any psychology teacher, whether newly qualified or experienced, whether working in a team or alone.

Dorothy Coombs, Chair – Association for the Teaching of Psychology (ATP)

Acknowledgements

The Publishers gratefully acknowledge the following for permission to reproduce copyright material. Whilst every effort has been made to trace the copyright holders , in cases where this has been unsuccessful or if any have inadvertently been overlooked, the Publishers will be pleased to make the necessary arrangements at the first opportunity.

'Reasons for choosing psychology' and 'Perceptions of interest value of psychology' adapted from 'Post-16 Student: Views and experiences of studying psychology' by S. Hirscheler and P. Banyard.

'Student and teacher rankings of interest factors' from 'Comparison of students and teachers mean rankings of importance of statements' by Kevin Walker. Copyright © Kevin Walker. Reprinted with the kind permission of the author.

'Psychology Undergraduates' beliefs about Post-16 Psychology' adapted from 'Second year undergraduate psychology students: views on their study of post-16 psychology' by M Linnell.

Zelchner & Tabachnick's classification of reflective practice taken from TEACHER DEVELOPMENT by Janet Soler, Anna Craft & Hilary Burgess, Paul Chapman 2001. Reprinted with permission of Sage Publications Ltd.

Extracts from 'Students entering higher education Institutions with Access Qualifications 2002–3' by Youell, HESA. From Higher Education Statistics Agency Student Record. Reprinted with permission of HESA.

Grade distributions by subject 2004 taken from DEPT OF EDUCATION AND SKILLS Copyright © Crown Copyright 2004. Used with permission.

Figure from Benjamin S Bloom Et Al, Taxonomy of Educational Objectives Published by Allyn & Bacon, Boston, MA Copyright © 1984 by Pearson Education. Adapted by permission of the publisher.

'The Holistic Critical Thinking Rubric' P. A. Facione and N. C. Facione HCTSR, Millbrae CA 94030: California Academic Press, 1994. Reprinted with the kind permission of the authors.

'Do as you're told' by Nicci Gerrard, from The Observer Review, 12th October, 1997 © Guardian Newspapers Limited 1997. Reprinted with permission.

'The Implicit Theories of Intelligence Scale (adult version) from 'Self Theories: Their Role In Motivation, Personality and Development' by C. S. Dweck, Psychology Press, 2000. Reprinted with permission of Taylor and Francis Inc.

Photo credits

Richard Bowlby (p. 89)

Introduction

Welcome! I hope that both new and experienced teachers of psychology will enjoy and get something useful from this book. My aim in writing it was to provide some practical suggestions to make life in the psychology classroom easier and more interesting, but also to set those same suggestions in a context of psychological theory and research – in other words to apply psychology to teaching psychology. This has meant drawing heavily on the published literature of psychology teaching. Some of the studies, models and strategies I refer to have been developed in the USA and some are adapted from work in Higher rather than post-16 education, however I believe that everything here is directly applicable to post-16 psychology teaching in the UK.

Inevitably some teachers reading this will be interested in sinking their teeth into the more esoteric issues, whilst many others will simply be looking for practical classroom ideas. Chapter 1 is very philosophical, as I consider issues like the appeal of psychology, what psychology can provide students with and what makes a good teacher. However, if you're primarily interested in practical stuff don't be put off – the book gets more applied as it goes on. In Chapter 2 I look at the psychology curriculum and provide some advice on how to choose a syllabus, defend the rigour of psychology and benchmark yourself properly. In Chapter 3 I look at what makes for effective teaching, using research and examples from the psychology teaching literature. Chapter 4 is concerned with strategies to help students to think 'psychologically'. In Chapter 5 I consider resourcing issues, including how to choose a textbook, what other sources of published literature to make use of and offer some hints for developing your own handouts and worksheets. Chapter 6 deals with information and learning technology (ILT), and I offer some ideas about a range of ways to incorporate technology into psychology lessons. Finally in Chapter 7 I look at diversity in the needs of psychology and make some suggestions for differentiation.

One thing I want to make very clear at the outset is the spirit in which the ideas presented here are offered. They are there to be drawn upon as required. There is no implication that we should all be doing all these things all the time, just that they may prove useful. If for example you are concerned about or want to further develop your use of ILT, you may find something helpful in Chapter 6. In these days of eroded teacher autonomy and sometimes oppressive quality assurance, it is important that teachers are armed with the sort of information that allows them to take a lead in developing professional practice. I hope this helps.

About the author

Matt Jarvis is a Chartered Psychologist, an experienced teacher of post-16 psychology and a Senior A-level examiner. He is also an experienced teacher trainer and education researcher. Currently he teaches psychology at Totton College and is a visiting lecturer in the Department of Education at Southampton University where, amongst other things, he teaches Continuing Professional Development courses for psychology teachers. Matt has served on the steering committees of the Association for the Teaching of Psychology and the British Psychological Society's Division for Teachers & Researchers in Psychology. He is a highly successful author in the fields of both psychology and education.

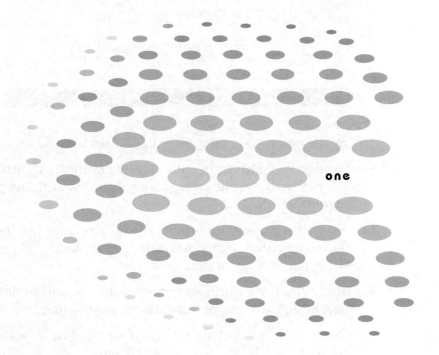

one

The philosophy bit: what are we here for?

The philosophy bit:
what are we here for?

learning objectives

By the end of this chapter you should be able to:

- Explain why students opt to study psychology with particular reference to the rigour, intrinsic interest and therapy hypotheses.

- Assess the potential benefits of studying psychology for students, with particular regard to transferable skills and preparation to study psychology at degree level.

- Apply research findings into reasons for and benefits of studying psychology to enhancing classroom practice.

- Outline the triad of attributes of an effective psychology teacher: subject knowledge, teaching skills and assessment expertise.

- Consider the concept of reflective practice as a model for understanding the developing psychology teacher.

- Discuss the role of evidence-based practice in psychology teaching and consider the psychology teacher as scientist-practitioner.

- Be aware of the breadth of ways in which psychology can be applied to teaching psychology.

This book contains a blend of theory, research and practical advice. If you are reading purely for the top tips you may prefer to skip this chapter. This is a chance to step back from the practicalities of the classroom to consider more broadly the philosophy of psychology teaching. This is not intended as an indulgence, but is rather based on the belief that practical ideas are born not necessarily from theory or research, but certainly from having a broader understanding of what we do. So what are psychology teachers here for? What do students seek from academic psychology? What makes any teacher effective? It is extremely difficult for any teacher to find the space in the teaching day to escape the minutiae of planning, teaching, marking and administering, and focus on these 'big picture' issues. It is however possible to at least consider these questions with reference to the psychology teaching literature.

A useful starting point is to consider why students opt to study psychology and what are the potential benefits of studying the subject. There is a respectable body of research addressing both these issues and some clear implications for shaping classroom practice. In order to achieve the ambitious range of goals suggested by this research I propose a triad of attributes that characterise an effective psychology teacher. In the remainder of this chapter I consider two rather different ways of thinking about the practice of psychology teaching: reflective practice and evidence-based practice. *Reflective* practice has become a byword for quality in education whilst *evidence-based* practice enjoys similar status in psychology. Psychology teachers, with a foot in each of these camps, are in the unique position of being able to appreciate and draw from the understandings of professional practice enjoyed by both disciplines.

Why do people study psychology?

The rapid growth in the popularity of psychology at post-16 and undergraduate levels has attracted considerable attention. Three major hypotheses have emerged from these discussions. *Rigour hypothesis* is the idea that psychology is, or is at least perceived by students as being, an 'easier' A-level, and so students choose it in the belief that they will gain a high grade with relatively little effort. *Intrinsic interest hypothesis* posits that psychology is seen as a particularly interesting subject, and that this interest is students' primary motivation. *Therapy hypothesis* emphasises the appeal of psychology to those seeking greater understanding of their own personal and mental health issues.

Rigour hypothesis

A recent suggestion from more conservative elements in the education establishment is that students see psychology as an easy A-level, and that this is important in accounting for its current popularity. We can call this the *rigour hypothesis*. Proponents of this argument cite a now-dated study by Fitz-Gibbon and Vincent (1994) showing that, at that time, students tended to score on average half a grade higher in psychology than in the most difficult subjects.

There is however wide agreement now that the rigour hypothesis is deeply flawed; apart from anything else the statistical evidence taken from more recent A-level cohorts is strongly supportive of psychology as a rigorous A-level (see Morris, 2003; Jarvis, 2004 and Chapter 2 for detailed discussions). Moreover, student surveys have found no evidence to suggest that students perceive psychology as an easy subject. On the contrary, Hirschler and Banyard (2003) report that 43% of post-16 students surveyed described psychology as more difficult than their other subjects, with 30% describing it as equally difficult and only 27% finding it easier.

Intrinsic interest hypothesis

In fact, studies have clearly shown that the overwhelming factor influencing students' choice of psychology is its fit with our current cultural ideas of what is inherently interesting. In one recent survey Hirschler and Banyard (2003) surveyed 454 post-16 psychology students (all but 17 studying A-level). Three factors emerged as particularly important in the decision to study psychology: interest, preparation for a career in psychology and the novelty value attached to a subject not previously studied. Table 1.1 shows the percentages.

In this study interest value emerged as the most popular response and no other factors were mentioned by more than 1% of respondents. Encouragingly, pre-study perceptions of psychology as an interesting subject were borne out by students' experiences. The majority rated it as more interesting than their other subjects. A breakdown of responses is shown in Table 1.2.

Walker (2004) has extended this line of research by breaking down further the idea of interest. Based on a content analysis of responses to the open question 'why do you want to study AS psychology?' Walker has identified five distinct aspects of interest:

- Interest in people (IP)
- Interest in subject matter (IS)
- Novelty interest (IN)
- Career interest (C)
- Personal issues (P).

Table 1.1 **Reasons for choosing psychology**

Rank	Primary reason	%
1	Sounded interesting	64
2	Want a career in psychology	19
3	Something different to study	11

Source: Hirschler and Banyard (2003)

Table 1.2 **Perceptions of interest value of psychology**

Response	%
Much more interesting	44
Slightly more interesting	36
About the same	15
Slightly less interesting	3
Much less interesting	2

Source: Hirschler and Banyard (2003)

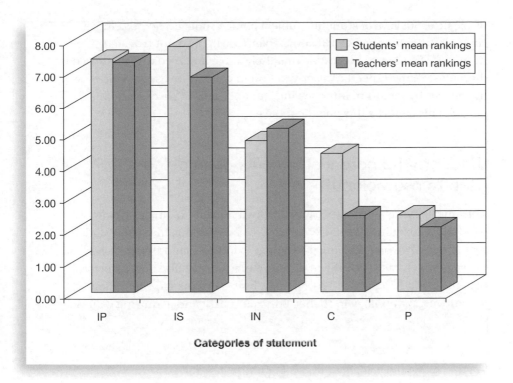

Figure 1.1 **Student and teacher rankings of interest factors**

When students and teachers were asked to rank these in order of importance there was a surprising level of agreement. Interest in people and subject interest emerged as the most important factors. Figure 1.1 shows student and teacher mean rankings.

Therapy hypothesis

It has long been believed by many post-16 psychology teachers that they have attracted a disproportionate number of students with mental health problems, and that these students have chosen to study psychology in an attempt – conscious or unconscious – to seek insight into their conditions. This has sometimes been called the *therapy hypothesis*. There is no doubt that many students with mental health problems do derive benefit from studying psychology, nor that for some this expected benefit is an important factor in their subject choice. However, there is little direct evidence that psychology attracts particularly large numbers of students with mental health problems. Teachers' folk beliefs concerning this may be an artefact of greater disclosure rates in the context of psychology where the lesson content cues disclosure. Surveys of students' subject choice-motives, such as those of Hirschler and Banyard (2003) and Walker (2004), have not revealed significant numbers of students suggesting that their subject choice was motivated by therapy-seeking. Indeed, Walker went on to directly investigate the therapy hypothesis by means of interviewing students, and in no case did his participants report a therapeutic motive.

What are the potential benefits of studying post-16 psychology?

This question has been approached from a number of angles in the psychology teaching literature. There is clear evidence that what students seek primarily from studying psychology is interest, and that in this sense they are widely satisfied. However, there may be additional long-term benefits of studying post-16 psychology, both in terms of preparation for studying psychology in Higher Education (HE) and acquiring generic skills.

Post-16 psychology and HE preparation

Until fairly recently there was a consensus that studying psychology at A-level was unhelpful in terms of preparation for study at undergraduate level, and that those seeking to study for a psychology degree should probably avoid psychology A-level. Although uninformed careers advisors still occasionally propagate this view the situation has changed dramatically in the last decade. With the vast increase in the popularity of post-16 psychology the preference of admissions tutors for applicants not to have previously studied psychology has become untenable. There is however still some ambivalence among HE teachers towards psychology A-level. One professor of psychology has spoken of the difficulty of teaching students 'acculturated into psychology A-level' (anon, personal communication). On the other hand, common sense suggests that students who have already studied psychology enter a degree with a better idea of what to expect.

In response to this lack of clarity the British Psychological Society undertook two studies, one involving HE teachers and the other students. In the first study Banister (2003) surveyed 27 Heads of Psychology from 25 UK universities regarding their perceptions of and policies towards post-16 psychology qualifications. In the majority of departments (15) post-16 psychology qualifications were not influential in the admissions process, although a minority (five) did specify that some psychology background was helpful for mature students. In a clear majority of departments (18) prior qualifications in psychology were neither encouraged nor discouraged. Perhaps the most interesting findings concerned the advantages or otherwise for psychology students of having a post-16 qualification. Although in raw figures students with psychology A-level did slightly worse on research methods and statistics courses than others, once GCSE and A-level score were controlled for they did slightly better (students with psychology typically had worse qualifications overall). There is thus some advantage in having a post-16 qualification for HE study. However, there was some concern expressed that students with a post-16 psychology qualification were at risk of coasting in their first year of undergraduate study and consequently adopting poor learning strategies thereafter.

Interestingly, these equivocal findings have been reflected in recent American research. Rossi, Keeley and Buskit (2005) compared the first year undergraduate performance at two universities of students who had studied psychology at high school level with those new to the subject. Despite an initial advantage at one of the universities for students with high school experience, by the end of the first semester there were no differences at either university between the two groups.

In the second BPS study Linnell (2003) surveyed second year undergraduate psychology students about their perceptions of pre-degree experience. Although attitudes were more positive amongst those who had previously studied psychology, overall students felt that post-16 psychology was helpful to studying undergraduate psychology. Percentages are shown below in Table 1.3.

Students in the Linnell study were acutely aware of the differences between post-16 and university teaching. Some commented that in the light of their university experience they now considered their earlier teaching poor. On the other hand others bemoaned the lack of opportunity for class discussion and the narrow focus on research methods and replicating classic studies required in undergraduate study.

Table 1.3 **Psychology undergraduates' beliefs about post-16 psychology**

Item	% yes (no post-16 qualification)	% yes (post-16 qualification)
Helped with study skills	61	92
Helped with understanding	78	94
Improved grades	67	78
Improved motivation	33	66
More enjoyable	48	76

Source: Linnell (2003)

Generic skills

The 1997 Dearing Report highlighted a need for the curriculum at post-16 and undergraduate levels to address more effectively the development of generic skills in students, as well as their subject knowledge. The current A-level psychology syllabi make reference to six key skills:

- Communication
- Application of number
- IT
- Working with others
- Improving own learning and performance
- Problem solving.

These broadly reflect the skills that psychology teachers expect to help develop during their teaching, with the exception of critical thinking, which is consistently rated as a transferable skill to which psychology is well suited (O'Hare and McGuinness, 2004), but which does not appear in Dearing's taxonomy of key skills. Communication, for example in report and essay writing, and application of number in the form of statistical analysis of research findings are perhaps particularly well suited for development through psychology. There is little research with which to evaluate how effective a vehicle post-16 psychology is for the development of these skills. Moreover, the introduction of key skills qualifications has meant that the transferable skills valued by psychologists are largely conflated with key skills as defined by Dearing, and are hence more difficult to study. Note however that in the Banister (2003) study (above) heads of university psychology departments believed that psychology was associated with good first year outcomes in statistics but not with good essay writing. This suggests that achieving good transferable skills cannot be taken for granted.

Hayes (1998) has taken a step back from considering the benefits of studying psychology to the individual and looked more broadly at the benefits for society of well-disseminated psychological knowledge and skills, including key skills but also higher thinking skills such as critical thinking, problem solving and awareness of alternative perspectives. Hayes suggests that the growth of communication of psychology to the general public has contributed to the shift away from 'simplistic, expert-driven forms of knowledge' (p. 52) towards the more sophisticated current understanding that issues can be thought of at different levels of explanation and that there is not always a single causal explanation for a phenomenon. Hayes identifies three strands through which psychological understanding has been transmitted to the public: psychology teaching, psychology media, including textbooks, and communication with other professions. As regards to psychology teaching – without the constraints experienced in degree-level teaching, where the primary aim is to prepare students for professional standards of research and practice in psychology – post-16 teaching has the freedom to focus on applying psychology to understanding real-life issues. This means that the generic skills acquired by post-16 psychology students, while less sophisticated than those of undergraduates, are also more readily applied to real scenarios and so have a profound ability to alter public consciousness.

Lessons from the research: what should psychology teaching give students?

Focus on the distal purposes of psychology teaching

Quality assurance mechanisms tend to encourage teachers to think exclusively in terms of outcome measures, such as achievement by grade percentages. Clearly grades are important and we would not be doing well by our students if we abandoned all exam preparation to pursue more esoteric ideals in the classroom. However, there are two factors mitigating against what I call the utilitarian model of psychology teaching, with an exclusive emphasis on drilling students for formal assessments. First, whilst psychology teaching has a *proximal* purpose in gaining the student a post-16 qualification, we are also responsible in some measure for what happens to students in the future – thus teaching also has long-term or *distal* purposes, most obviously in the form of transferable skills. Thus whilst it is possible to gain students good coursework marks by rushing them through a formularised process, this is unlikely to instil a deeper understanding of the research process, nor does it foster the best report-writing skills. An opportunity to foster transferable skills is therefore lost and the distal purpose not achieved. Second, and pragmatically of greater value to teachers engaged in performance management, utilitarian processes of exam drilling are likely to detract from student motivation, and so not facilitate their aim of optimal achievement. To get the most from students it is essential that they receive the things psychology promises at the outset.

Make psychology interesting and relevant

This is in some ways so obvious that it may appear crass. Most students take up psychology for the sake of interest and the majority do find it interesting. However, this does not mean that every topic is always taught in such a way as to maximise its interest value, nor that every option is equally interesting to students. Experience suggests that in general it is theory and research with a clear real-world implication or application that arouses student interest. Every time a theory is taught, given a finite limit on the total volume of information students should take away, there is a trade-off to manage between level of theoretical detail and the time left for real-world implications/applications. To maximise the interest value that can be obtained from a topic, try to avoid thinking 'how much theoretical detail should I teach for students to have the sort of understanding I'd like?' and think instead 'how little turgid theoretical detail can I get away with teaching if students are to have a satisfactory understanding?' The latter approach may help free up time to focus on making the topic interesting, which in turn will probably lead to its being deeper processed and better remembered. The theme of how to maximise the interest value of psychology is a recurring one in this book. Examples of strategies include applying theory and research to understanding real-life scenarios (see page 51) and making reference to popular culture, for example in psychoanalytic interpretation or content analysis of television programmes (page 97).

Consider the needs of students going on to psychology degrees

In the Linnell (2003) survey study a number of undergraduate students reported that they found the transition from post-16 to undergraduate level difficult and would have welcomed more support. It was also clear that opinion varied as to how useful post-16 psychology was as a preparation for a psychology degree. Banister (2003) reported that studying post-16 psychology was less associated with good essay skills than was studying other subjects. In the current psychology A-level specifications following Curriculum 2000, essay writing now assumes less importance than was the case in the traditional pre-2000 A-levels. In terms of preparation for HE this is unfortunate. It is clear then that we cannot assume that post-16 teaching necessarily constitutes effective preparation for HE. Of course responsibility for the post-16–degree transition does not lie exclusively with post-16 teachers, and it can be difficult to reconcile the proximal aim of preparing for A-level exams with the more distal aim of preparing a minority of students for a psychology degree. Nonetheless, there are some things that post-16 teachers can do to lessen the culture shock of moving to Higher Education. Some examples are shown in Box 1.1.

If you are concerned about preparing students for a psychology degree but these activities seem too radical a departure from your usual teaching, consider writing a short tailored course for future psychology undergraduates. The Open College Network accredits short courses of at least 30 notional hours and OCN accreditation makes courses fundable. You may well find that your local university will be supportive of any efforts to smooth the post-16-HE transition and help design such a course.

Box 1.1

Strategies to better prepare post-16 students for a psychology degree

- Prepare students to use electronic resources. Psychology undergraduates will use library databases to locate books, specialised databases like PsycINFO to find original studies and statistical packages like SPSS to analyse data. Much of this software is beyond school and college budgets but there are similar and very user-friendly freeware packages with which post-16 students can become familiar (see Chapter 6 for details).

- Expose students to a range of texts that represent the same material differently and which express contrasting views. Part of the 'acculturation' that concerns some HE teachers occurs because at post-16 level it is possible for students to think of what is in their textbook as 'fact'. At undergraduate level they will have to recognise that each textbook contains merely a representation of the original material presented and evaluated in the light of the author's interpretation and biases.

- There are other ways to encourage students to think beyond textbook contents. Doug Bernstein, former Chair of the National Institute on the Teaching of Psychology (NITOP), has pioneered a useful exercise in which he gives groups of students the task of summarising studies described in his textbooks and showing students how different their interpretations of the study are to his own and to each other's (Bernstein, personal communication).

- Expose students to some psychology journals. Although journal papers are initially intimidating to anyone, mostly because of the statistical analyses, it is possible with appropriate scaffolding for students to extract much more detailed information about studies from original papers than from textbook accounts of them. A useful exercise is to present students with papers (carefully selected for conceptual level) from which the abstracts have been removed and have students generate their own abstracts.

- Focus on teaching psychological thinking throughout the course. For example, rather than teach evaluation points for theories and studies, focus on teaching *how* to evaluate theories and studies. This develops the transferable skill of critical thinking. Strategies to achieve this are discussed in Chapter 4.

- Expose students to academic psychologists. Many lecturers are happy to give talks in schools and colleges. Remember as well that academics are often short of research participants, and that your students can gain valuable experience of seeing 'real' research in action by serving as participants. See Chapter 3 for a model of how this has been achieved.

What makes an effective psychology teacher?

Of course, the answers to this depend on what as psychology teachers we are seeking to achieve. Based on the literature reviewed so far it is clear that psychology teachers can aspire to a range of goals (after Perlman and McCann, 1999):

- To get students the highest grade possible
- To teach students about the subject matter of psychology
- To enthuse students about psychology
- To teach students to think like psychologists
- To use psychology to teach generic skills
- To use psychology to understand the world.

These differing responses reflect a (healthy) tension between academic excellence, idealism and pragmatism. So what factors might impact on teachers' ability to meet these aims? There are now available numerous taxonomies of teacher skills and competencies (see for example Kerry and Wilding, 2004). The following is a relatively simple model for characterising the profiling of the effective psychology teacher:

- Subject knowledge and skills
- Generic and subject-specific teaching skills
- Assessment regime expertise.

Subject knowledge and skills

It is a truism that effective teaching requires a minimum level of subject knowledge. This includes both knowledge of the subject and the skills that go with it, for example research design and critical thinking. Of course, some teachers will be professionally qualified psychologists whilst others will have little or no background in psychology. In a survey for the British Psychological Society's report on post-16 psychology teaching (Jarvis, 2003), a substantial minority of psychology teachers – 28% of school teachers and 19% of FE lecturers – did not have an HE qualification in the subject. This is absolutely *not* to suggest that psychology teachers without a psychology background cannot be effective teachers. This finding does however highlight a direction for professional development – 100% of the report's sample who did not have psychology degrees reported that they would undertake a suitable qualification in psychology if it existed.

A further dimension of subject understanding that has aroused some debate in the psychology teaching literature concerns our shared (or otherwise) understanding of the nature of psychology – notably its status as a science. Kimble (1999) has criticised the introductory psychology curriculum on the grounds that its very diversity fails to instil in students a shared scientific ethos. By contrast, Sternberg and Grigorenko (1999) have praised this breadth, pointing out that it reflects the nature of the discipline and that outstanding psychologists do not conform to a narrow set of standards. Moon (2001) has attempted to reconcile this argument by recommending that diverse areas of psychology be taught but that they should be understood in terms of a scientific understanding. In other words, science should be the bottom line, but that rather than science being a rigid standard, it should be understood from the outset that there are good reasons why some areas of psychology are not studied from the standpoint of traditional science.

Generic and subject-specific teaching skills

There are numerous classifications available of the generic skills and competencies required by teachers. This literature raises numerous debates that are not within the scope of this book, however it is worth looking briefly at one particularly influential taxonomy from Hay McBer (2000), published under the auspices of the DfES. Hay McBer identify the following generic skills as one of three components of effective teaching (the others being professional characteristics and classroom climate):

- Lesson-flow
- Planning
- Class management
- Assessment
- High expectations
- Methods and strategies
- Time and resource management
- Homework.

On reading this book it will become clear that, whilst generic teaching skills are important, there are in addition a number of subject-specific techniques developed for psychology teaching. Some of these have not been widely disseminated amongst post-16 psychology teachers and they represent an important direction for professional development in experienced teachers. Examples include Sternberg's triarchic model of psychology teaching (page 78), Norton's use of psychology applied learning scenarios (PALS) (page 51) and McGhee's work on developing psychological thinking skills (page 72).

Assessment regime expertise

This refers not to the generic skill of assessing student progress during courses but specifically to the understanding teachers need to develop of the processes by which the outcomes of their courses will be assessed. For most post-16 psychology teachers this will mean understanding the assessment procedures followed by the unitary awarding bodies responsible for psychology A-level. Some of these are discussed further in Chapter 2, and a number of training providers, including the exam boards themselves, learned bodies such as the Association for the Teaching of Psychology, and private training companies, provide workshops on A-level teaching, conduct of coursework and marking. However, there is no substitute for first-hand experience, and the best way to gain an in-depth understanding of the exam system is probably to become an assistant examiner or coursework moderator. Most teachers report after their first experience of examining that they have a better understanding of how to prepare students for exams and some rethink much of their practice.

Professional visions of the psychology teacher

If we have established a range of goals for psychology teaching and explored some of the attributes of the psychology teacher that contribute to their achievement, perhaps the next logical task is to look at how the psychology teacher can achieve those attributes. Two models are of particular interest, reflecting the dual professional identity of the psychology teacher. The *reflective professional model* has been particularly influential in education. The *scientist practitioner model* dominates applied psychology.

The psychology teacher as reflective professional

For a more detailed account of reflectivity see Jarvis (2005). What follows here is a condensed version of that discussion. A broad vision widely espoused by educationalists has been of the teacher as a 'reflective professional'. The term captures effectively the essence of teaching as having professional status and the teacher as an active participant in both individual professional development and as a contributor to wider pedagogical development.

The most influential view of reflective practice comes from Schon (1983, 1987). Schon has proposed a complex model of professional expertise by fusing cognitive and social-constructionist theory. Based on social-constructionist awareness, Schon proposed that professions entered a crisis by the 1980s due to the growing awareness of the limitations of *technical rationality*, the dominant belief that professional ability could be understood simply in terms of mastering a set of skills. Based on a cognitive understanding of automatic processing of information (Allport, 1980; Tharp and Gallimore, 1991) Schon developed the term 'knowledge in action' to describe the ability of the experienced professional to respond automatically to a situation without diverting attentional resources and distraction. Rather than subscribing to technical rationality, Schon suggested that professional expertise could be better understood in terms of 'professional artistry', whereby experienced professionals make use of knowledge in action.

To Schon the reflective professional is distinguished by the capacity to consciously bring to bear a subjective awareness of their knowledge in action. This means that actions that would otherwise be implicit and automatic become explicit and can be reflected upon individually and shared in a process of professional discourse. Much of this reflection occurs simultaneously with the action, thus the reflective professional is constantly analysing and modifying their practice. This is called *reflection in action*. This is not, as has been sometimes suggested, to devalue the automatic processing involved in responding to situations in the form of teachers' craft knowledge, but rather to suggest that conscious reflection upon these automatic processes is an effective tool of professional development.

Schon's ideas have been enormously influential in educational academia. The concept of reflectivity has enormous *heuristic* value (i.e. as a cognitive tool to aid thinking about a topic) amongst those seeking to look at development of pedagogy. Amongst practitioners the term 'reflective practice' has also proved something of a rallying cry for those seeking to improve the professional status of teachers and has been linked closely with Schon. This is not to say that Schon is without critics. Usher *et al.* (1997) have pointed out a logical inconsistency between reflection in action as a *feature* of professional practice and deliberate attempts to *apply* Schon's model by demonstrating reflectivity. Those influenced by Schon can only try to apply the model and, by definition, this cannot be to achieve Schon's ideal. In addition, Schon's liberal mix of cognitive and social-constructionist principles is epistemologically messy, fusing theoretical ideas based upon largely incompatible views of the nature of knowledge and human understanding.

Since Schon's seminal work there have been a number of attempts to develop the reflectivity construct. Zeichner and Tabachnick (2001) have offered a much broader view of reflectivity, outlining four perspectives from which to understand reflective practice in education. These are shown in Box 1.2.

This classification has the advantage of breadth, encompassing a role for planning, application of research and consideration of the individual needs of the learner. It also serves as a useful template for education professionals wishing to develop their capacity for reflection after action. However, appealingly simple and comprehensive as this classification system appears,

Box 1.2

Zeichner and Tabachnick's classification of reflective practice

- **The academic perspective**: concerned primarily with reflection on subject matter
- **The social efficiency perspective**: concerned with reading and applying education research
- **The developmentalist perspective**: concerned with reflecting on the needs of learners
- **The social reconstructionist perspective**: concerned with reflecting on the broader socio-political context of education.

there are potential limitations. On one hand, its very breadth takes away precision from the term *reflectivity*. Is the psychology teacher who prepares elaborate lessons with careful use of both their subject knowledge and teaching skills demonstrating reflectivity or simply good planning? Can the teacher who pays particular attention to catering for the needs of a learner with an unusual learning style or learning difficulty be said to be *reflective* or rather sensitive and responsive? Certainly this broad definition of reflectivity moves away from Schon's use of the term, particularly as most 'reflection' in this broad sense takes place outside the classroom and cannot be seen in terms of reflection in action. The acknowledgement of the socio-political backdrop to education certainly suggests a *thoughtful* professional, but not necessarily one engaged in reflection on refining their practice.

The psychology teacher as scientist practitioner

If reflectivity has been the dominant idea in understanding the teacher as professional then the professions of applied psychology have been similarly dominated by the scientist-practitioner ethos. Essentially, this means that the psychologist is trained as both a practitioner and researcher, and that research and practice are integrated in the sense that the practising psychologist contributes to research and subscribes to evidence-based practice, i.e. they try as far as possible to use techniques that have been validated by research. The British Psychological Society's Division for Teachers and Researchers in Psychology (DTRP) promotes the ideal of linking teaching and research in its stated aims 'to ensure that the essential mutual relationships between teaching and research – so special within psychology – are sustained wherever psychologists are engaged in teaching; and to promote the application of psychological knowledge in the settings where psychological research is conducted and psychology is taught' (British Psychological Society, 1997).

There are serious problems in attempting to crudely emulate the scientist-practitioner ethos as it applies to other areas of applied psychology. One problem – felt even in clinical practice where the role of psychologist is distinguished from other therapeutic professionals by the science-practice link – is that the scientist-practitioner label can seem precious and elitist (Shapiro, 2002). This could present considerable problems for psychology teachers in the face of the egalitarian ethos of the staffroom. Moreover, evidence-based practice is currently made difficult by the inadequate volume of directly relevant research. Indeed, education research as a whole lacks rigour in comparison with comparable disciplines (Hargreaves, 1996) and relevance to practitioners (Hillage *et al.*, 1998), in comparison with that on which applied psychology is based. These problems are compounded by the tendency for evidence-based techniques to be disseminated in a top-down manner, meaning that teachers often lack a sense of ownership.

Clearly then neither the state of the evidence base nor the context in which psychology teachers operate are conducive to adopting a strict scientist-practitioner ethos. However, there is no reason why teaching should not be informed by research, provided teachers have realistic expectations and retain a sense of ownership of their practice. The more politically neutral term 'research-informed psychology teaching' is now used to gently promote the influence of empirically validated technique (Zinkiewicz, Hammond and Trapp, 2003). Actually there are some compelling reasons for psychology teachers to at least dip into the research literature of psychology teaching and to consider contributing to that literature.

1. Accounts of techniques used successfully elsewhere can inspire the teacher to broaden their own professional understanding and practice. This is true even when research has been conducted in a different context, e.g. USA schools or UK universities. This is *not* to suggest that teachers should make knee-jerk responses and change their teaching to follow evidence-based practices, just that perusing research *can* inspire innovation.

2. In the current era of quality assurance teachers have increasingly to justify their practice. Being able to refer to published evidence is a powerful argument for doing things your way! This is especially the case when you can demonstrate personal expertise by means of citing your own publications.

3. The term 'evidence-based practice' is being spoken with increasing frequency in government circles in relation to education. In light of the growing expectation that teaching methods will conform to the empirically verified, there is a real danger that teacher discretion and hence professional status will be eroded. Top-down direction of teaching methods can only be resisted if teachers actively contribute to the evidence base, demonstrating that in fact they 'know best'. Psychotherapists, a decade or so ahead of teachers in facing this issue, have responded by supplementing the top-down evidence-based practice agenda with a bottom-up agenda of *practice-based evidence* (Barkham and Mellor-Clark, 2000).

4. Researching your own practice is likely to lead to an enhanced understanding of what happens in your classroom. Psychology teachers, with a degree of disciplinary knowledge of research methods, are well placed to research their own practice. Moreover, as Nummedal, Benson and Chew (2002) point out, consideration of what works in teaching and learning should be intrinsically interesting to proponents of psychology – a discipline largely devoted to establishing cause and effect relationships. More pragmatically, conducting this type of research is recognised as continuing professional development and can form part of performance management.

5. Whilst the current evidence base for psychology teaching is limited, we can work towards a more substantial body of evidence and cautiously begin to identify techniques that can be said to be reliably demonstrated to work in the context in which psychology teachers work. For example, a technique demonstrated to work well in an American university department of sociology *may* prove effective in the psychology A-level classroom of a UK school. If we ignore it on the basis of the context in which it originated we may be missing a trick. Clearly, though, we cannot take it as read that the same technique will benefit practice in our very different context. The logical way to respond to such a technique would be to replicate and evaluate it in the psychology classrooms of UK schools and colleges.

Applying psychology to teaching psychology

This can be considered as an aspect of evidence-based practice in the wider sense that we can apply an empirically validated psychological theory to teaching psychology, even when such theory may not have been validated specifically in the context of teaching psychology. Zinkiewicz, Hammond and Trapp (2003) have suggested a range of ways in which disciplinary knowledge of psychology can be applied to teaching psychology. These are summarised in Table 1.4.

Clearly the application of psychology to teaching psychology is tremendously broad and we cannot do justice to it in this short section. Many of the areas identified by Zinkiewicz and colleagues form the basis of discussions in this book. For those particularly interested in developing this area of their practice the British Psychological Society provides a diploma in the applied psychology of teaching psychology. Details can be obtained from the British Psychological Society website.

Table 1.4 Examples of applying psychology to teaching psychology

Area of psychology	Examples of applicable theory and research
Cognitive development	Piaget's genetic epistemology, Vygotsky's sociocultural theory, and research into adult cognitive development
Student diversity	Intelligence and ability, personality, learning styles, cultural diversity
Learning and thinking	Behavioural theory, experiential theory, cognitive approaches, theories of memory and learning
Motivation	Intrinsic and extrinsic motives, humanistic theories, cognitive theories
Social processes	Group development, conformity, intergroup relations, attitude change and leadership
Barriers to and facilitators of learning	Arousal, anxiety and stress Psychotherapy and resilience

After Zinkiewicz, Hammond and Trapp (2003)

Summary and conclusions

Students overwhelmingly opt to study psychology because it fits neatly with our current cultural understanding of what is intrinsically interesting. There is little empirical support for alternative explanations for psychology's increasing popularity. As well as a qualification students have the opportunity to gain from post-16 psychology a set of transferable skills and a possible advantage in studying psychology at degree level. However, neither of these benefits should be taken for granted, and it is important that teachers are aware of both making the subject interesting as well as engendering transferable skills. This raises the question of teacher effectiveness. We can think of the effectiveness of the psychology teacher in terms of three dimensions: subject knowledge and subject-specific skills, teaching skills, and expertise in the assessment process. Two visions of the professional are particularly important in understanding how psychology teachers can develop their practice. The reflective professional model is particularly influential in teaching, whilst the scientist-practitioner model is similarly influential in psychology. Whilst both of these models have their limitations they are helpful in pointing to directions for continuing professional development.

Self-assessment questions

1. Critically consider the reasons why students choose psychology. What implications do these reasons have for professional practice?

2. To what extent does post-16 psychology help students beyond their course? What can teachers do to influence the long-term benefits of studying psychology?

3. What makes a psychology teacher effective?

4. What are the benefits of research-informed psychology teaching?

5. Outline the range of ways in which psychology has been applied to teaching psychology.

Further reading

•••••• Hayes, N. (1998) Can teaching psychology transform popular culture? *Psychology Teaching Review*, **7**, 44–54.

•••••• Jarvis, M. (2005) *The Psychology of Effective Learning and Teaching*. Nelson Thornes, Cheltenham.

•••••• McGuinness, C. (ed) (2003) *Post-16 Qualifications in Psychology*. British Psychological Society, Leicester.

•••••• Zinkiewicz, L., Hammond, N. and Trapp, A. (2003) *Applying Psychology Disciplinary Knowledge to Psychology Teaching and Learning*. LTSN, York.

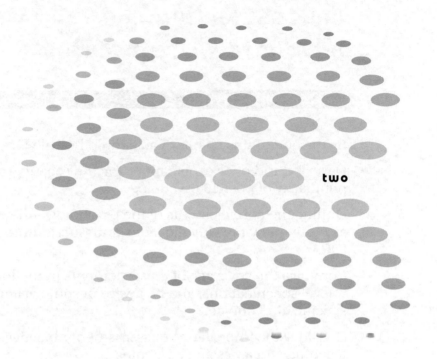

two

Understanding the psychology curriculum

Understanding the psychology curriculum

By the end of this chapter you should be able to:

- Describe and offer explanations for the recent growth in the popularity of post-16 psychology.

- Outline the core elements of the psychology A-level curriculum as outlined by the Qualifications and Curriculum Authority (QCA).

- Compare the coverage of these elements in the four psychology A-level specifications, and be aware of some criteria affecting specification choice.

- Consider the importance of assessment objectives (AOs) in teaching and assessing psychology.

- Be aware of additional post-16 qualifications in psychology including AEA, Access to HE and SQA Higher.

- Discuss the rigour of psychology A-level in comparison to other subjects.

- Understand the role of benchmarking in assessing department performance and how to obtain and use appropriate benchmarks.

At the time of writing, psychology at post-16 level is growing at an unprecedented rate. In particular, A-level numbers are increasing at almost 20% a year. The main purpose of this chapter is to better understand the psychology curriculum. The Qualifications and Curriculum Authority (QCA) has set down a set of core elements of psychology A-level. However these are broad and open to interpretation. This has meant that, in contrast to some subjects where the specifications of different awarding bodies are almost indistinguishable, there is a very healthy contrast between the content and approaches of the four psychology A-level specifications currently available. I say 'healthy' because this diversity allows psychology teachers an opportunity to exercise a degree of professional discretion in choosing the specification that best meets their abilities and the needs of their students. It would be inappropriate in a book like this to attempt to influence teachers' choices in this area but it is worth comparing specifications and discussing the criteria that might affect teachers' decisions.

A second aim of this chapter is to look at some current issues in the management of psychology curricula. One of these is the rigour of post-16 psychology – this is important in the light of recent media coverage that suggests that 'newer' and 'trendy' subjects (psychology is certainly both of those) are easier than more traditional disciplines. Another is the assessment of psychology teachers and departments using benchmark data. Both of these are issues on which psychology teachers may be required to defend themselves. I have sought to arm teachers with the necessary information to deal with both of these.

The growth of psychology A-level

The growth of A-level psychology over the last decade is phenomenal. By 2003 it was the third most popular A-level subject (Morris, 2003). Numbers of AS and A-level candidates across the four exam boards are shown in Table 2.1.

As we might expect, AQA specification A, formerly the syllabus of AEB, being the oldest and best established of the syllabi has the greatest market share. Edexcel, as a relative newcomer, has the smallest numbers, though it is the fastest growing (see Table 2.3). The percentages of students continuing from AS to A2 range from 60.25 (AQA specification A) to 70.40

Table 2.1 **Numbers of candidates taking psychology A-level Summer 2004**

Board/specification	AS numbers (2004)	A2 numbers (2004)
AQA spec A	45,900	27,658
AQA spec B	8,221	5,788
OCR	12,921	9,007
Edexcel	7,300	4,540
Total	74,342	46,993

Source: the awarding bodies

Table 2.2 **Progression from AS to A2 2004**

Board/spec	% progression to A2
AQA A	60.3
AQA B	70.4
OCR	69.7
Edexcel	62.2
Overall	63.2

Source: the awarding bodies

(AQA specification B), with an overall figure of 63.21%. Figures for each specification are show in Table 2.2.

We should of course be very cautious about reading too much into the comparisons between the progression rates of the different specifications as there are likely to be confounding demographic differences between the students studying each syllabus. Although psychology A-level numbers were increasing steadily during the 1990s they have exploded since the advent of Curriculum 2000. Figures showing the growth in AS numbers since 2001 are shown in Table 2.3.

A further development in recent years has been the movement of psychology into the school sector, post-16 psychology having being traditionally located in further education (FE) colleges. Most students of A-level psychology are now school-based. The proportions of students located in schools and colleges are shown in Table 2.4 (OCR does not keep this data).

In general, as we would expect given the typical prior achievement of students entering school sixth forms and FE colleges, a higher proportion of top grades are found in students in school sixth forms. This is demonstrated in Table 2.5, which compares the grade distributions for Edexcel A-level for

Table 2.3 **Growth of psychology by board from 2001 to 2004**

Board/specification	AS numbers 2001	AS numbers 2004	% increase
AQA spec A	30,446	45,900	50.76
AQA spec B	5,790	8,221	41.99
OCR	8,299	12,921	55.69
Edexcel	3,763	7,300	93.99
Total	48,298	74,342	53.92

Source: the awarding bodies

Table 2.4 **Distribution of psychology AS-level students across school and college sectors**

Board/specification	% students in schools	% students in colleges
AQA spec A	56.80	43.20
AQA spec B	53.38	46.62
Edexcel	77.83	22.17

Source: Edexcel and AQA

Table 2.5 **Distributions of Edexcel psychology A2 grades by sector 2004 (%)**

Grade	A	B+	C+	D+	E+	U
School	17.0	39.2	63.0	81.6	93.6	6.4
College	10.5	30.7	55.0	79.4	93.0	7.0

Source: Edexcel

June 2004 in schools and colleges. Note that there is little difference in A–E pass-rates but that there are substantial differences in the A–C rates. These differences are important when it comes to assessing your department against benchmarks – clearly a single benchmark figure can obscure substantial sector effects. This is discussed further onpage 36.

Factors affecting the growth of psychology

There is no single definitive answer to why psychology has grown so much in popularity and there is currently little directly applicable empirical research. The following are offered as some likely factors.

- **Growth of psychology-related careers**: Numbers of applied and academic psychologists are currently increasing. For example, Lavender, Thompson and Burns (2003) report that since 1980 the number of training places in clinical psychology has increased by 309%. Numbers doubled between 1992 and 2002, making clinical psychology the fastest growing health profession. This means that, in contrast to previous 'glamour subjects' like sociology, post-16 psychology delivers on its promise of a clear progression pathway through first degree to a professional qualification as an applied psychologist.

- **Changing cultural perceptions of scientific interest**: The increase in numbers of students opting for psychology has gone hand in hand with a decline in the numbers seeking to study traditional sciences, in particular physics and chemistry. A range of reasons has been suggested for this shift, including poor science teaching in schools and perceptions of traditional sciences as particularly difficult. However, one factor is certainly a perception of traditional sciences as 'dry' and lacking in intrinsic interest. Psychology by contrast is seen as of tremendous interest (Hirschler and Banyard, 2003; Walker, 2004).

- **Glamorous media representations of psychology**: The most obvious example is Jimmy McGovern's *Cracker*, which ran from 1993 to 1996. Since then it has become *de rigueur* for police dramas to feature a forensic or clinical psychologist. These psychologist characters are accorded tremendous status. When a forensic psychologist was criticised on *The Bill* by a cynical CID officer, a colleague expressed outrage: 'You can't talk about him like that . . . he's a Chartered Psychologist!' Popular literature has similarly become awash with hero-psychologists, notably Jonathan Kellerman's *Alex Delaware* and James Patterson's *Alex Cross*. As well as adding to the popular representation of psychology as intrinsically interesting, characters like these have provided role models to which students can aspire.

25

- **The shift to four subject choices**: Prior to Curriculum 2000 it was standard practice to take three subjects at A-level. However, since 2000 the vast majority of AS-level students study four subjects. This has led to students being more adventurous in choosing a non-National Curriculum fourth subject. This has combined with the growth of public interest in psychology and perceptions of psychology as glamorous to boost its popularity.

These three suggestions, while difficult to test directly, are based on solid data, including growing numbers of applied psychologists, declining numbers studying traditional sciences and increasing numbers of psychologists portrayed in glamorous roles in the media. Additional factors have been proposed but these are rather more speculative. For example, one suggestion is that the growth of psychology has gone hand in hand with a decline in church attendance, psychology providing a culturally appropriate secular belief system. Another is that increasing disillusion with the school curriculum is leading young people increasingly to opt for subjects, such as psychology, which they have not studied previously.

The core A-level curriculum and the specifications

Based on the British Psychological Society's Qualifying Examination categories, the Qualifications and Curriculum Authority set out terms of reference on which the Curriculum 2000 specifications were based. QCA specified that AS and A2 specifications were to include five broad areas:

- Cognitive psychology
- Biological psychology
- Social psychology
- Developmental psychology
- The psychology of individual differences.

In addition all the A-level specifications make reference to research methods, themes and debates, and critical thinking. Using these areas as a vehicle, A-level specifications are designed to achieve a set of educational aims, laid down by QCA. These are shown in Box 2.1.

Prior to Curriculum 2000 there existed three psychology A-level syllabi, run by three of the four English exam boards: AEB, NEAB, and Oxford and Cambridge. The Boards were restructured into three unitary awarding bodies: OCR (formerly Oxford and Cambridge), AQA (an amalgamation of AEB and NEAB) and Edexcel (formerly London Board). In 2000 OCR and AQA launched new specifications that, whilst conforming to the new QCA criteria, were designed to capture the essence of their pre-2000 A-level syllabi. At the same time Edexcel launched a new psychology specification. In spite of the

Box 2.1

QCA requirements for psychology A-level specifications

AS and A level psychology specifications encourage students to:
- Study psychological theories, research, terminology, concepts, studies and methods
- Develop skills of analysis, interpretation and evaluation
- Develop an understanding of different areas of psychology
- Design and report psychological investigations, and analyse and interpret data
- Develop an understanding of ethical issues in psychology, including the ethical implications of psychological research.

In addition, A-level psychology specifications:
- Include the study of psychological principles, perspectives and applications
- Enable students to explore and understand the relationship between psychological knowledge, theories and methodology, and their relationship to social, cultural, scientific and contemporary issues
- Enable the study of cognitive, social and physiological psychology
- Enable the development of critical and evaluative skills in relation to theory, empirical studies and methods of research in psychology
- Enable candidates to have an understanding and critical appreciation of the breadth of theoretical and methodological approaches in psychology.

27

common elements specified by QCA each of the current psychology specifications has a distinct content and character.*

The AQA A specification

This is the oldest, best-established and perhaps the most traditional of the specifications. The AS-level consists of three examined units. These are intended to cover the core areas of cognitive, developmental, biological and social psychology and individual differences. Each topic has a critical issue designed to allow students to apply theory and research to real-life issues. The A2 specification develops the core areas further. In addition the A2 requires a detailed consideration of perspectives on psychology, as well as a project brief and 2000-word report of a psychological investigation.

* The specifications can be downloaded in full from the awarding body websites. Web addresses are provided in Appendix IV.

The AQA B specification

In its pre-2000 manifestation this is the next oldest specification. The AS-level consists of two examined units and a 1500 word write-up of a psychological investigation. Unit one covers theoretical perspectives with particular emphasis on biological approaches, research methods and gender, while unit two addresses social and cognitive psychology. Unit four consists of child psychology and one applied psychology option: health psychology, atypical behaviour or contemporary topics. Unit five assesses perspectives, debates and research methods. Unit six is a second investigation.

The OCR specification

This is one of the younger specifications and arguably the most radical in approach. The emphasis at AS-level is on classic published studies, units one and two specifying 20 core studies covering the core areas specified by QCA. In addition to the core studies students are expected to be aware of the approaches and key elements of relevant theory and critical issues (for example attachment and child care in developmental psychology). Unit three consists of an exam based on a practical folder comprising four research activities: a questionnaire, an observation, an experiment and a correlation. At A2 students opt for two areas of applied psychology from a choice of education, health, organisational, environmental, sport and criminological. They also complete a psychological investigation.

The Edexcel specification

This is the newest specification. The emphasis at AS-level is on theoretical perspectives, with unit one covering social, cognitive and cognitive-developmental approaches, and unit two learning theory, psychodynamic and physiological approaches. Unit three consists of a 1500 word report of a psychological investigation. At A2 students opt for three areas of applied psychology in units four and five, options being child, health, environmental, clinical, criminological, sport and educational. In addition research methods and perspectives, issues, and debates are examined.

Assessment objectives

To fully understand the aims of the Curriculum 2000 developments and the A-level specifications we need to be familiar not just with specification content but with assessment objectives. There are three assessment objectives (AOs) underlying the formal assessments made in AS and A2 level exams and coursework. They reflect different aspects of psychological thinking, discussed further in Chapter 4. The AOs are phrased slightly differently in the four specifications. The following is intended to summarise and clarify the assessment objectives across all specs.

- AO1: **Knowledge and understanding**. Students need to demonstrate *knowledge* in the form of clear and accurate description of psychological material, including concepts, principles, theories, perspectives, studies, applications and methods. *Understanding* is demonstrated by selecting the concepts, theories etc. to answer a question, and by explaining the meaning and significance of findings.
- AO2: **Analysis, application and evaluation**. These represent higher thinking skills (see page 63 for a discussion). *Analysis* involves going beyond a basic understanding to see causes, problems, solutions and consequences. This is what was referred to as 'commentary' under the old AEB scheme. *Application* involves taking a psychological study, theory, concept, etc. and using it to explain a real-life situation or to predict what might happen in a given situation. Students are also required to demonstrate the skill of *evaluation*, i.e. identifying strengths, weaknesses, contributions and limitations of psychological concepts, theories, studies, methods and applications.
- AO3: **Research skills and methodological awareness**. These represent the skills and understanding needed to pursue primary research in psychology. Students need to know how to plan, design and carry out primary research and to report their investigations including a presentation and analysis of their data.

Choosing a specification

If you are new to teaching psychology the chances are that you will not have been given any choice in which specification you teach to. However, it is instructive to at least be aware of the differences between the four, and of course you may find yourself in the position of having to choose in the future. All the specifications have their loyalists and their detractors. This would not be the case if any of the four were entirely lacking in virtue! In that spirit, rather than comment on the alleged strengths and weaknesses of each specification I offer a set of criteria to consider.

1. How interesting will your students find the content? Given that the intrinsic interest value of psychology is the most important factor in students' choice of psychology, it is important to consider how interesting they will find the content of their specification.
2. A related question concerns the extent to which each specification lends itself to a range of interesting teaching methods. *How* as well as *what* you teach will impact on the quality of students' experiences.
3. How do you perceive the discipline of psychology? Different specifications have different emphases on research methodology, studies, theory and application. Your personal emphasis will affect your perception of the educational value of each specification.

4. How applied do you think a psychology course should be? Different specifications have very different emphases on traditional academic and applied psychology.

5. What do you think constitutes good preparation for a psychology degree? The four specifications have varying degrees of similarity to the first year undergraduate syllabus. You may believe that a similar or dissimilar A-level specification will be of greater benefit to students progressing to degree level.

6. Do different specifications provide differing levels of opportunity to develop transferable skills in your students? You might want to consider differing emphases on essay-writing or conducting primary research.

7. How transparent and appropriate do the assessment methods of each awarding body appear to you? Look at past exam papers and mark schemes or examiners' reports to get an idea of which Chief Examiner's thinking you are most in tune with.

8. What is the content-load of each syllabus? Consider the number of teaching hours you have available for each AS and A2 group. Look at how each specification would divide up week by week and consider how able are your typical students. You might favour one specification if you have highly selected students for six hours a week and a different one altogether if you have more mixed ability students for four hours a week.

Other post-16 psychology qualifications

Access to HE

Access courses are tailor-made courses, broadly equivalent in level to A-levels, designed to meet the needs of mature students returning to study and seeking to enter Higher Education. They have existed for around 20 years, but have recently seen a significant growth in numbers. Courses generally include a range of subject options, psychology being a popular choice. Since 2002 Access courses have been kite-marked by the Quality Assurance Agency (the HE body approximately equivalent to QCA). Courses are now unitised under the Open College Network and units can either be written by teachers and accredited by an Open College Network or bought 'off the shelf'. Access units vary rather more than do A-level units because they have varying emphases on content and study skills development. Be aware of this when choosing or writing Access units – some courses are much more content-heavy than others. The latest statistics from HESA (the Higher Education Statistics Agency) show that Access students do roughly as well in degrees as do A-level students, with slightly fewer attaining 1st class and upper 2nd class degrees, but fewer failing.

Table 2.6 **Degree classifications of Access students vs others (%)**

Entry qualification	1st	2:1	2:2	3rd/pass	Fail
Access	8.28	41.98	36.40	9.40	3.45
Other	10.56	45.41	32.27	7.18	4.56

Source: Youell (2003)

SQA qualifications

Since 1999 the Scottish Qualifications Authority (SQA) has offered psychology at four of its five levels: Intermediate 1, Intermediate 2, Higher and Advanced Higher. The Higher has been regarded as the 'gold standard' for university entry and is roughly equivalent to AS-level. Levels 1, 2 and Higher consist of three mandatory units: understanding the individual (early socialisation, memory and stress); investigating behaviour (research methods); and the individual in social context (including social psychology – prejudice, anti-social behaviour, conformity and obedience relationships, and individual differences – intelligence and abnormality). The Advanced Higher (A2 equivalent) consists of two mandatory units, perspectives and research methods, and a choice of one of five specialisms in developmental, cognitive, social, biological psychology or individual differences. By 2004, 2779 students took the Higher in psychology. Numbers are increasing at a slower rate than is true of A-level psychology, at a rate of around 13% a year.

Advanced Extension Award (AEA)

The first AEA in psychology was launched by AQA in 2004, being first examined in 2005. AEAs have replaced S-levels as an extension qualification designed to stretch the most able candidates. According to QCA there has been considerable interest in AEAs from the universities, and from 2006 they carry UCAS points, 40 for a distinction and 20 for a merit. The psychology AEA aims to encourage students to:

● Apply psychological concepts, theories, approaches and research methodology creatively and in novel situations;
● Evaluate information and evidence about how psychology can be used and applied in society;
● Bring together and use knowledge of the ways in which different areas of psychology relate to each other;
● Understand and evaluate the range of methods and techniques used by psychologists to collect and analyse information;
● Communicate knowledge and understanding of psychology coherently and effectively.

There is no specification above and beyond A-level, and AEAs are designed to be suitable for students who have studied any of the A-level specifications. Assessment is by means of a single three-hour exam including three sections:

- Section A: One compulsory structured question. Interpretation, analytical and evaluation skills.
- Section B: One compulsory structured question. Understanding psychological methodology.
- Section C: One essay question from a choice of three. The application of psychological knowledge.

The rigour of psychology A-level

With the tremendous growth in the numbers of students taking A-level psychology, the subject has come under increasing scrutiny, and more conservative elements in the education establishment, notably John Dunford of the Secondary Heads' Association, have made highly disparaging comments about the rigour with which psychology A-level is assessed. Dunford's notorious assertion that psychology is easier than maths is reportedly based on a study by Fitz-Gibbon and Vincent (1994), which showed that students undertaking psychology A-level alongside more traditional subjects typically did better in psychology than in their other subjects and that, when GCSE profile was controlled for, students of psychology achieved better grades than students with comparable grades undertaking traditional subjects. This was a methodologically sound study, to be taken seriously if not accepted uncritically, however the social and educational context in which A-levels are taken has changed considerably in the last decade, with a proportionate impact on the grade distribution across subjects (Morris, 2003). More recent data paint a rather more balanced picture. For example, data for A-levels taken in 2002 from the Curriculum, Evaluation and Management Centre shows that, when GCSE results are controlled for, the UCAS points achieved by students taking maths and psychology are very similar, both falling in the centre of the distribution of A-level subjects (see Figure 2.1). This suggests that psychology and maths are of comparable difficulty (Jarvis, 2004).

Psychology teachers who enjoy a friendly rivalry with colleagues in sociology will enjoy the fact that by this criterion psychology emerged as significantly the more difficult of the two! Another approach to comparing the rigour of psychology with more traditional A-levels is to look at their grade distributions. Tables 2.7 and 2.8 show some variation in the distribution of grades across the four specifications. Table 2.10 shows the distributions of grades across a range of subjects.

It is apparent that there are significant differences in grade distributions between specifications. There are also some year-on-year variations (see Table 2.9). As with sector effects, these variations become important when it

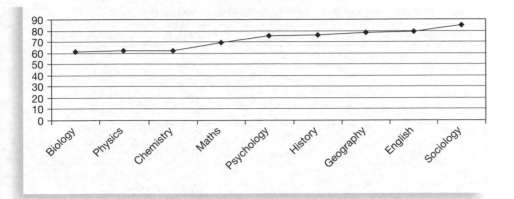

Figure 2.1 UCAS points achieved by students in 2002

Adapted from data from the CEM Centre

Table 2.7 A-level grade distributions by board 2004 (%)

Specification	A	B+	C+	D+	E+	U
AQA spec A	18.3	40.0	63.2	82.4	94.4	5.6
AQA spec B	18.7	41.2	63.7	82.6	94.5	5.5
OCR	16.7	43.1	69.7	87.5	96.8	3.2
Edexcel	15.8	37.8	61.5	80.9	93.3	6.7

Source: the awarding bodies

Table 2.8 AS-level grade distributions by board 2004 (%)

Specification	A	B+	C+	D+	E+	U
AQA spec A	13.2	27.6	45.5	63.7	71.7	29.3
AQA spec B	14.3	30.6	48.8	66.0	81.2	19.8
OCR	15.4	37.2	60.5	78.7	90.5	9.5
Edexcel	13.6	32.8	53.7	71.7	85.3	14.7

Source: the awarding bodies

Table 2.9 **Year-on-year variation in A-level pass rates (%)**

Board/specification		2002	2003	2004
AQA spec A	A–C	58.8	61.5	63.2
	A–E	92.7	93.6	94.4
AQA spec B	A–C	57.9	60.3	63.7
	A–E	92.3	93.2	94.5
OCR	A–C	60.1	68.7	69.7
	A–E	94.4	96.2	96.8
Edexcel	A–C	57.0	61.7	61.5
	A–E	92.4	94.5	93.3

Source: the awarding bodies

comes to assessing your department against benchmarks. This is discussed
further on page 36.

It is apparent from Table 2.10 that psychology A-level has a relatively low
pass rate and a significantly lower proportion of higher grades than some
more traditional subjects, suggesting that it is a relatively difficult subject.
Further evidence to support the rigour of psychology A-level comes from
student surveys, which suggest that psychology is typically perceived as at
least as difficult as respondents' other subjects. Hirschler and Banyard (2003)
surveyed 454 post-16 psychology students (92% of whom were studying
AS/A-level) about their perceptions of the difficulty of psychology. Table 2.11
shows the percentages of respondents believing psychology to be easier,
equivalent to or more difficult than other subjects.

In this sample, the modal response was that psychology was perceived as
more demanding than the subjects taken alongside it. Responses were similar
when students were questioned regarding the workload in psychology and
their other subjects. Of course, student responses alone are not particularly

Table 2.10 **Grade distributions by subject 2004 (%)**

	A	B	C	D	E	U
Psychology	17.8	22.7	23.8	18.9	11.5	5.3
English	20.6	23.7	27.1	19.6	7.4	1.6
Modern languages	42.6	30.3	14.6	6.6	3.2	2.7
Maths	37.7	21.3	16.5	11.7	7.8	4.8
Physics	28.4	20.7	18.8	15.2	10.9	6.0
Chemistry	29.9	24.1	19.0	13.8	9.0	4.2
All subjects	22.4	23.4	23.2	17.5	9.5	4.0

Source: *Education Guardian*

Table 2.11 **Student perceptions of the difficulty of psychology**

Level of difficulty	% of respondents
Psychology more difficult	43
Psychology equally difficult	30
Psychology less difficult	27

Adapted from Hirschler and Banyard (2003)

solid evidence, but taken in conjunction with the grade distributions and average UCAS points they help paint a picture of psychology as a highly rigorous A-level.

The 'dumbing down' argument

A final criticism that can be countered by statistical evidence concerns the general 'dumbing down' of A-level exams. This is a common criticism as A-levels have adapted to an agenda of widening participation. Given that general cognitive ability is normally distributed throughout the population and that a much wider spectrum of candidates are undertaking advanced level study this is a legitimate research question (Rust and Golombok, 1999). However, it is essential that the importance of an issue does not lead us to prejudge the outcome. It may be that changes to A-levels have been qualitative rather than quantitative, reflecting greater transparency and a reduction in bias towards the cultural capital of middle class students. In any case the dumbing down argument is based on the assumption that as the number of candidates increases so does the proportion of low-ability candidates. This is an entirely inappropriate basis on which to challenge psychology A-level given that, whereas until around 10 years ago psychology was predominantly offered in FE colleges, it is now an important part of the sixth form curriculum, where standards are typically higher (Morris, 2003).

A related issue to 'dumbing down' is grade inflation. Certainly it is clear from Table 2.9 that in three of the four A-level specifications the A–C and A–E rates have risen each year. This is a legitimate concern as A-level pass-rates in general are fast approaching 100%. However, it would be a mistake to assume from this statistic that the rigour of assessment is declining. The Curriculum 2000 A-levels are now several years old, and over that time teachers have adapted to their demands, becoming more skilled at preparing students for the new-style assessments. Resources have improved over that period, with a wider range of textbooks and more internet sites devoted to post-16 psychology.

Since the mid 1990s the Qualifications and Curriculum Authority (QCA) has maintained a rolling programme of checks of the maintenance of standards across time within subjects at GCSE and A-level. QCA (2001) published a review of the examination of psychology A-level between 1977 and 1997, looking at both examination and grade standards. Although the report highlighted some changes in the style of questions in the intervening period (for example questions had become more explicit) and some disparities between the standards required by the examination boards at Grade E, it was concluded that both standards of exam difficulty and performance were maintained. In the absence of evidence to the contrary it seems reasonable to believe that standards in psychology A-level have been maintained.

Using benchmark information

It is now standard quality assurance practice to compare psychology departments in schools and colleges against national benchmarks. Whilst it is inherently tempting to see 'how one is doing' by looking at this type of data, by virtue of our disciplinary knowledge psychology teachers are in a position to look critically at the data we are judged against. It is tempting to see a benchmark as a gold standard against which we must fare well. However, there are a number of ways of obtaining benchmark figures, and benchmarks can vary considerably according to their origins. When presented with a benchmark figure, critically consider it in the light of the following:

- Is the figure you are given up to date? There are some year-on-year variations in grade distributions, and although trends are generally upwards this has not been true every year for all specifications. If for example your students follow the Edexcel specification and you obtained an A–E rate of 94% in 2004, but the benchmark you were judged against was from 2003 (94.5%) you would be judged as scoring below average. In reality you would have achieved marginally above the national A–E percentage of 93.3 for 2004.
- Does the figure you are given refer to the specification you take? There are substantial variations in the grade distributions for different specifications (see Tables 2.7 and 2.8). If for example you are given a benchmark for A–C A-level achievement based on OCR figures (68.7% for 2003, 69.7% for 2004) and you in fact obtained 65% A–C you would appear to be doing less well than the national average. In fact if your students followed any of the other specifications 65% would be above the national average.
- Does the figure you are given refer to your sector? There is some variation between schools and colleges, particularly in A–C rates. If you work in an FE college check that your benchmark figures are not derived from school sixth forms, which typically have higher achievement.
- Do you have separate benchmark figures for male and female achievement, or is the figure you receive adjusted for the proportion of male and female students you teach? Girls' achievements outstrip

those of boys in psychology to a much greater extent than in most subjects,* so if you have a higher percentage of boys than the national average for your specification and this is not taken into account you may well be disadvantaged.

The quality of benchmarks supplied to schools and colleges is increasing. However it cannot necessarily be relied on. Accurate benchmark information, referring to your sector and specification, and showing male and female norms, can be obtained from the websites of the awarding bodies.

Summary and conclusions

Psychology at post-16 level, in particular A-level, has grown at an unprecedented rate in the last five years. Factors affecting this probably include the shift in cultural norms of intrinsic interest and the resulting glamorous media representations of psychologists. Since 2000 A-level psychology specifications are written to a set of core criteria laid down by QCA, and are examined on a common set of assessment objectives. However, the four A-level specifications each have a distinct character of their own. All the specifications are growing steadily in numbers and all have loyal supporters. The criteria for choosing a spec are personal, relating to teachers' perceptions of the fit between each spec and their beliefs about psychology and their intuitive understanding of the thinking of the examiners.

There have been questions asked about the rigour with which 'newer' and fashionable subjects are assessed at post-16 level. In the case of psychology, data from a number of sources, including UCAS points of students undertaking different subjects, grade distributions and student perceptions suggest that psychology is rigorously assessed. Another issue facing psychology teachers concerns benchmark data. Be aware of the variable quality of benchmarks available and be sure that you obtain the up-to-date figures that pertain to your specification and sector.

Self-assessment questions

1. How and why has psychology grown so much in popularity as a post-16 subject?

2. Outline the core psychology curriculum and explain how this is interpreted differently in the four A-level specifications.

3. How might a teacher choose between the four A-level specifications?

4. What evidence is there to support psychology A-level as a rigorously assessed A-level?

---

* See Chapter 7 for a detailed discussion of gender and achievement.

5. How can you be sure you are comparing your success rates against the correct benchmarks?

Further reading

•••••• http://www.aqa.org.uk/qual/gceasa/psyA.html

•••••• http://www.aqa.org.uk/qual/gceasa/psyB.html

•••••• http://www.ocr.org.uk/OCR/WebSite/docroot/qualifications/qualificationhome/ showQualification.do?qual_oid=2065&site=OCR&oid=2065&server= PRODUKTION

•••••• http://www.edexcel.org.uk/quals/gce/psych

•••••• Jarvis, M. (2004) The rigour and appeal of psychology A-level. *Education Today*, **54**, 24–28.

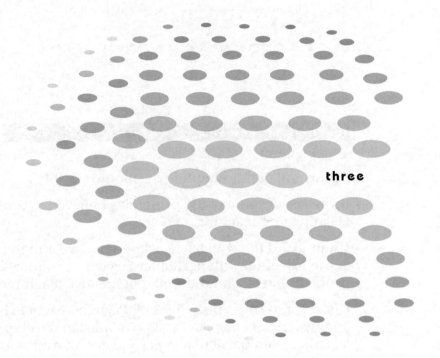

three

Four principles of effective learning and teaching

Four principles of effective learning and teaching

By the end of this chapter you should be able to:

• Be aware of some of the principles believed to underlie effective learning and teaching.

• Understand the constructivist perspective and the importance of active learning, with particular regard to enquiry-based, problem-based and multiple-perspective teaching.

• Understand some principles of social constructivist education and use social constructivist principles to develop interactivity in learning, with particular regard to collaborative learning and peer tutoring.

• Appreciate the importance of making psychological material relevant to students, for example by means of Psychology Applied Learning Scenarios (PALS) and experiential learning.

• Outline some principles of information processing theory and discuss the importance of structuring material and practising recall by means of tests and quizzes.

• Discuss the use of metacognitive strategies for exam preparation.

There has been for many years substantial literature generated about the 'correct' or 'best' way to teach. However, while this has encouraged healthy debate and innovation, relatively little consensus has emerged, and fashions in teaching can change very rapidly. Moreover, there is always a complex interaction between teaching strategies and the characteristics of the individual teacher, the topic and students, both as individuals and groups. This means that while there may be a best way for one teacher to teach a particular topic to a particular class (this is usually more obvious in retrospect!), we would be very unwise to say that there is a single best approach to teaching psychology as a whole.

It is important to be clear at the outset that the aim of this chapter is *not* to prescribe a particular model of teaching. Nor is it even to suggest that effective teaching is primarily a matter of implementing a set of techniques – research has shown unequivocally that students rate the quality of their relationship with their teacher as more important than their choice of pedagogical techniques (Jarvis, 2005). The much more modest aim of this chapter is to present a range of psychological principles and lines of research and practice in the belief that all teachers, however experienced and competent, may benefit from considering both the rationale underlying what they already do and the possibility of extending their current practice.

Without favouring a particular approach to teaching, it is possible cautiously to draw from the range of contemporary theory and research a set of basic principles that can be said to underlie effective learning and teaching. There are perhaps six such principles that we can say are important in affecting the quality of teaching and learning.

1. Learning should be an active process. High levels of student involvement can be achieved in a variety of activities, including whole-class, small-group and independent exercises. It is a common misunderstanding that students are only active if they are working without input from a teacher.

2. Learning can be enhanced by appropriate social interaction. This interaction can be with a teacher or peers, or even with software, and can take place in a range of whole-class or small-group exercises.

3. Learners are likely to be most active in their learning when the subject matter is inherently relevant to them or made so by teaching. Thus teaching should involve applying research and theory to real-life scenarios.

4. Learning needs to be well remembered. However much emphasis we place on the distal purposes of teaching, such as developing transferable skills and preparation for studying psychology at higher levels, there is a proximal aim to prepare students for assessment, which is primarily by means of exams.

5. Learning is as much about developing skills, including more advanced ways of thinking, as it is about mastering a set of facts.

6. Teaching must take account of the diverse needs of learners.

Developing psychological thinking and catering for student diversity warrant their own chapters. The remainder of this chapter is devoted to applying psychological theory and research to developing the first four principles in teaching psychology.

1. Making learning active: the constructivist position

The constructivist tradition owes much to the ideas of Jean Piaget, but is inextricably linked to the ideas of other pioneers such as John Dewey. To post-16 psychology teachers, Piaget will forever be inextricably linked to a stage model of cognitive development. However, Piaget's work was much broader than this, suggesting a distinctive approach to understanding learning. Piaget put great emphasis on human curiosity and saw learning as an active motivated process in which we constantly construct successively more complex understandings of the world. The concept that perhaps distinguishes Piaget's view of learning from alternative approaches is *agency*. To Piaget agency referred to the human motivation to actively pursue knowledge, in other words to be the agents of our own learning. This active learning is stimulated by a state of *disequilibrium* or *perturbation*, the uncomfortable sensation of not understanding a situation. As we pursue knowledge of a topic we construct successively more advanced mental representations of it – hence the term 'constructivist'.

Although it is possible for students to be fully engaged in active learning in whole-class activity, for example when discussing or debating an issue, the emphasis in constructivist education has been on shifting practice away from whole-class didactic teaching, in which the teacher takes the active role and students a generally more passive role, towards student-centred activity in which learners pursue topics independently. Sizer (1992) puts it thus: 'The governing practical metaphor of the school should be student-as-worker rather than the more familiar teacher-as-deliverer-of-instructional-services' (1992: p. 226).

To put it simply, constructivist lessons involve students finding things out for themselves – what we might call 'discovery learning'. The role of the teacher is to set up tasks that stimulate students to want to learn about a topic and forces them to think deeply about it, for example by testing hypotheses or pursuing alternative lines of enquiry. An appropriate task will stimulate perturbation and so motivate learning. Forcing the learner to think in different ways facilitates the construction of successive mental representations of the topic. Only student-centred tasks that stimulate perturbation and encourage students to employ their reasoning abilities are truly constructivist. Simply setting the task of note taking from a book may have some benefits in the form of varying lesson pace and encouraging students to read their textbook, but without some additional 'twist to the plot' in order to stimulate interest and require the exercise of reasoning, it is not truly in the spirit of constructivist teaching.

Problem-based and enquiry-based learning

Dahlgreen and Dahlgreen (2002) distinguish between two related approaches to constructivist learning. Problem-based learning (PBL) involves students considering how to use psychological material to solve a tightly defined problem. Enquiry-based learning involves more open tasks, for example preparing debates or presentations on a topic. Both these approaches involve students being presented with a task that involves actively searching for psychological material, selecting from it and applying it to achieve a goal. Both can be carried out individually or collaboratively, using department book stocks, libraries and the internet. Enquiry-based learning has the advantage of giving the student more freedom to focus on material that stimulates their interest and suits their style of learning (Palmer, 2003). Problem-based learning can have the advantage of focusing students on tightly defined topics, important at A-level where there is little time available to diverge from the specification. Boxes 3.1 and 3.2 show examples of enquiry-based and problem-based learning in the psychology classroom.

Box 3.1

Examples of enquiry-based tasks

- Prepare a presentation on one theory of forgetting, including its supporting evidence.
- Produce a poster on the importance of attachment for a child's development.
- Produce a leaflet on effective stress management that a GP might put in his or her waiting room.
- Set out the arguments for either the role of biological factors or psychological factors in one mental disorder.
- Locate a set of ethical guidelines from the website of the British Psychological Society or the Association for the Teaching of Psychology, and use it to assess the ethics of Milgram's studies of obedience.
- Using your textbook, find a detailed account of one laboratory experiment. Evaluate it in terms of its ecological validity, replicability and practical applications.

Box 3.2

Examples of problem-based tasks

- The victim of a crime has wrongly identified you. Use studies showing that eyewitness testimony in general and specifically face recognition can be inaccurate to make your defence.
- Your local nursery is losing business because of newspaper reports that day care is bad for children's development. Prepare a report challenging this idea that the nursery can show potential parents.
- A local firm is losing money because its workers are taking so much time off because of work-related stress. Offer the firm advice on what aspects of people's jobs can cause work-related stress and what strategies it might use to tackle the problem.
- A character in a television soap opera is being treated unfairly because his or her behaviour is unusual and eccentric. Your friends ask you as the psychology student to explain the arguments for and against deviation from social norms as a basis for defining someone as abnormal.
- Social psychology experiments are extremely interesting, but often raise ethical issues. You could not, for example, replicate the Milgram procedure as a student practical. Design or find an example of a published study in the area of obedience or conformity that would be ethically acceptable.

Multiple-perspective tasks

Cook (2005) suggests that a further way to force students to actively construct advanced mental representations of a topic is to approach the topic from multiple perspectives. Psychology lends itself to this approach because for almost any phenomenon or scenario we can use alternative theories or wider theoretical perspectives to explain what is happening and why. Box 3.3 shows an example of how several social-psychological theories can be used to explain the Holocaust. Box 3.4 shows an example of how alternative psychological perspectives can be used to explain an everyday clinical problem. Note that in both these examples there are multiple cues to guide students towards particular theories and theoretical approaches. Note as well that information has to be not merely retrieved but applied in order to complete the task.

Box 3.3

Multiple-perspective task one: an example of using theories

Genocide involves the deliberate and systematic attempt to wipe out a group of people. The best-known historical example of genocide is the Holocaust. In 1940s Nazi Germany, under the leadership of Adolf Hitler, over 6,000,000 people, including Jews, Romanies, trade unionists and people with physical and mental disabilities, were rounded up, sent to concentration camps and murdered. Ordinary people knowingly participated in this process. Hitler was reportedly a highly persuasive speaker, who spent considerable time in speeches emphasising the group identity of the Aryan race and the inferiority of out-groups. The Nazi regime was characterised by the use of visible symbols of authority and the encouragement of highly formal status-based styles of interaction.

Suggest how each of the following theories might provide a partial explanation of the Holocaust.
1. Social identity theory
2. Authoritarian personality theory
3. Agency theory
4. Charismatic leadership.

Box 3.4

Multiple-perspective task two: an example of using psychological approaches

Nigel works in an office. He is rather shy and does not feel confident to socialise with his colleagues. Sometimes people take advantage, for example giving him extra work to do, and he tends not to deal with them effectively. One day four colleagues are talking about him and suggest different explanations for his behaviour.
A. It's probably because he had an unhappy childhood. His dad died when he was a child and his mum is really odd.
B. He's just never learned how to act around other people. He never had a male role model and his mum punished him whenever he tried to stick up for himself.
C. He always looks on the downside of everything. He doesn't notice when people are nice to him and he said once that he couldn't remember the last time he had a friend.
D. He's never had the space to grow or be himself. He'd flourish in the right environment.

E. He was probably born like that. People have a certain type of brain and that's that.

F. It's not fair to just look at him as an individual. This office is always really bitchy, and there's a culture here of putting down anyone a bit different.

(a) Match each of these explanations of Nigel's behaviour to the following theoretical approaches to clinical/abnormal psychology: humanistic, behavioural, psychodynamic, social, biomedical, cognitive.

(b) Suggest how a psychologist might use each of these approaches to help Nigel.

Adapted from Wilkinson and Campbell (1997)

2. Making learning interactive: the social constructivist position

The social constructivist position derives from the work of Lev Vygotsky (see Jarvis, 2005 for a review). Note that this approach is very much compatible with the constructivist position – there is simply an additional emphasis on the role of social interaction during learning. Enquiry-based, problem-based and multiple-perspective tasks can be carried out on an individual or co-operative basis. Vygotsky conceived of learning as taking place between a learner and a more advanced peer or adult instructor. He conceived of knowledge as existing initially on an *intermental plane* (i.e. between two people) and only then on an *intramental plane* (i.e. in the mind of the individual). The difference between what a student can understand working alone and what he or she can potentially understand through interaction with others is called the *zone of proximal development* (ZPD). The teacher or advanced peer guides the learner through the ZPD in a process called *scaffolding*. From the social constructivist perspective the key to effective learning activity is the establishment of purposeful on-task interactions in which one-way or two-way scaffolding can take place. Strategies to establish this type of interaction include collaborative learning and peer tutoring.

Collaborative learning

This can take the form of pair or small-group work. The types of tasks suitable for collaborative learning are not necessarily much different from those that lend themselves to individual active learning. However there are additional variables to consider because of the group format. Meyers (1997) suggests three aspects of collaborative learning to be considered:

- **Task structure**: the nature of the task should be amenable to group work, i.e. it must *either* divide up so that each student can take responsibility for one aspect, *or* include problems that students can solve through discussion. For example, multiple perspective tasks work well for groups because each group member can take responsibility for one perspective. For tasks where division of labour is less obvious more substantial teacher input is helpful.

● **Student evaluation**: if marks are to be recorded for the group task we need to be clear in advance how they are to be allocated. Individualised identification of performance may reduce social loafing, however a collective mark may encourage group cohesion.

● **Group structure**: various strategies can be used to encourage a group to work well together. Drawing on social identity research, Carlsmith and Cooper (2002) suggest that naming groups, encouraging them to sit together in class and sending them to separate areas to work can all increase group cohesiveness.

The limitations of collaborative learning are well documented, and in spite of its potential advantages in terms of encouraging on-task interaction, many commentators believe that these are outweighed by practical difficulties. One problem is timing. By virtue of the time taken to research information, constructivist tasks generally tend to take longer than didactic teaching and this can be exacerbated in collaborative learning when groups spend time negotiating roles, responsibilities and strategies before commencing a task. This can be tackled by imposing a structure on a group, i.e. allocating tasks. Social loafing is a further issue, as collaboration gives the opportunity for less motivated individuals to participate less actively than would be the case in individual activity. A meta-analysis by Karau and Williams (1993) suggests that social loafing is least in evidence when the following conditions are met:

● When participants believe that their individual contribution can be identified and assessed
● When the task is important or meaningful
● When the group is cohesive
● When individuals believe their own contribution is significant to the end result
● When the group is small.

The jigsaw technique

A variation on traditional collaborative learning is the jigsaw technique. This makes use of structured worksheets to provide a certain proportion of necessary information, saving research time and focusing student efforts on aspects of the task that require actively using the information. By dividing up elements of the task between group members or whole groups it becomes possible to cover substantial volumes of material in no more time than would have been required for didactic teaching. An example of a lesson using the jigsaw technique to teach media violence is shown in Box 3.5. This lesson can

Box 3.5

Using the jigsaw technique to teach media violence

1. Explanation is provided of social learning theory as a basis for proposing a link between media violence and aggressive behaviour.
2. The class is divided into three groups. Each group has a different A3 worksheet outlining one method for researching the effects of media violence (e.g. case studies, prospective studies and experimental studies). These provide details of studies and ask questions requiring analytical thinking (e.g. in the light of research into the characteristics of effective role models, why might fears that the ankle-stabbing scene in *The Evil Dead* might inspire copycat crimes have been unfounded?) and critical thinking (e.g. what are the limitations of case studies such as the James Bulger murder as evidence for a link between media violence and aggressive behaviour?). The groups jointly answer these questions.
3. After a break in which the teacher produces A4 copies of the completed worksheets for all, students individually fill in a pro forma media violence sheet selecting studies and comments from the photocopies.

be completed in an hour, certainly no longer than needed for a lecture covering a range of methods used to research the impact of media violence.

Perkins and Saris (2001) provide evidence for the effectiveness of the jigsaw technique. They divided an undergraduate statistics class into four groups, each completing a different part of an analysis of variance (ANOVA) test. Student evaluations suggested that the jigsaw technique was an efficient use of class time and enhanced understanding of statistics. A quasi-experimental comparison of student evaluations of the course before and after introducing the jigsaw technique suggested that it significantly enhanced the student experience.

Peer tutoring

A related strategy involving structured interaction between learners is peer tutoring, in which a more advanced learner takes on the tutor role in order to assist a less experienced or less able peer. This replicates the type of interaction that characterises siblings, in which younger children can be observed to develop more rapidly than their older brothers and sisters because of the availability of scaffolding from a more advanced child (Dunn and Munn, 1985). Peer tutoring has been applied to a huge range of age groups, from primary school children to adults in Higher Education.

An example of the use of peer tutoring in post-16 psychology comes from Oley (2002). Sixty-five American students aged 17+ took part. They were set a five-page essay that required considerable background research. In one condition they worked independently. In another peer tutoring was provided. In a third condition peer tutoring from more experienced students was made available as an option. Irrespective of whether peer tutoring was forced or optional, students benefited from having a peer tutor. Grades were significantly higher and a positive correlation emerged between grade and time spent with peer tutor.

A practical problem to overcome in the use of peer tutors comes in the form of finding the tutors. In the American system, in which the Oley study took place, tutors were offered course credits. In the UK this is not applicable, however there may be some mileage in writing Open College Network (OCN) submissions for short courses in tutoring and marketing these to experienced students, such as those on A2 courses, on the basis of gaining teaching experience. Level 3 OCN courses carry UCAS points as well as providing students with useful work experience. See the NOCN website for details of how to write and gain accreditation for this type of course. The web address at the time of writing is http://www.nocn.org.uk/members/prog-accred.html.

Box 3.6

A checklist for assessing topic delivery for activity and interactivity

		YES	NO
1	Are there tasks in which students locate information for themselves?		
2	Is there problem-based learning?		
3	Is there enquiry-based learning?		
4	Are there multiple-perspective tasks?		
5	Are students required to think analytically or critically?		
6	Are there tasks that require students to select material for themselves?		
7	Are there collaborative tasks involving division of labour?		
8	Are there collaborative tasks involving joint problem solving?		
9	Are there opportunities for one-to-one coaching of students?		
10	Are there opportunities to provide scaffolding contingent on student progress?		
11	Are there jigsaw tasks?		
12	Is there formal peer tutoring?		
13	Are there opportunities for students to work with peers of different ability?		
14	Is whole-class teaching genuinely interactive?		

3. Making learning relevant: selecting and applying psychological material

It has been a cherished factoid amongst teachers for many years that 'it doesn't matter what you teach, it's how you do it that counts'. In one sense this is true; what students take away from post-16 psychology is a set of skills including quite advanced ways of thinking. They will not remember the details of most of the theories and studies you cover in class. However, where there is discretion on a syllabus to choose material it is well worth considering what topics, theories, studies and examples you will use on the basis that some are inherently more relevant to the lives of students. Recall from Chapter 1 that the most powerful factor affecting students' decision to study psychology is that it is inherently interesting (Hirschler and Banyard, 2003; Walker, 2004). Clearly, the more relevant material is to students the more they will engage with it and the more actively and interactively they will pursue an understanding of it. Relevance can be achieved in several ways.

Topic options

Consider student interest in choosing subject options. For example in the AQA spec B A2 specification there is an inherently interesting option to study 'contemporary topics'. This gives an opportunity to study parapsychology, substance abuse, relationships and criminological psychology. In Edexcel and OCR A2 specs there are a range of applied psychology options, some of which, for example criminological psychology, are often of particular interest to students because they have particular contemporary cultural relevance.

Use of up-to-date material

Consider introducing up-to-date material. There has long been a healthy tension between psychology teachers (at all levels) who emphasise traditional material and those who favour the use of more up-to-date material, in particular studies. Clearly if we omit seminal studies students miss out on understanding the development of a field. Thus there is a strong case for retaining a degree of traditional material. However, the major advantage of using some more recent studies is that they tend to be more relevant to students. There are for example fascinating and accessible contemporary studies of eyewitness memory looking at the 9/11 attacks, and studies of helping behaviour that show discrimination against gay people and supporters of rival football teams. These never fail to stimulate lively discussion. Similarly, discursive theory applied to explaining prejudice generally stimulates a debate over the merits of 'politically correct' language. Fitting in this contemporary material necessarily means cautiously looking for traditional material that can be dropped.

Use of news stories

Use relevant media stories, in particular those that catch the imagination of students, to bring theory to life. An example of a dramatic media story in 2005 was the coverage of the Michael Jackson trial. This has been widely used as a vehicle to illustrate the psychodynamic principle of the importance of early family relationships for later development. Earlier in the year the debate over censorship of Premier League football was used to illustrate social learning theory and the possible effects of media violence. These types of stories lend themselves to internet-mediated enquiry-based learning tasks or to the production of worksheets. A newspaper article can be used as stimulus material on which questions can be based requiring students to apply theoretical understanding to explain an event or debate. Suggestions for sourcing relevant news stories are made in Chapter 5.

Psychology Applied Learning Scenarios (PALS)

Psychology teaching at all levels has long involved the application of psychological theory and principles to real life scenarios. Recently this has been formalised (Norton, 2004) into the notion of PALS. A PALS is a vignette around which will be set one or more tasks designed to stimulate thinking and apply psychological principles and/or theory. As well as bringing life-relevance to psychological theory PALS encourage psychological thinking and active learning. Norton's work has been concerned primarily with degree-level psychology, however the technique is applicable to post-16 level. PALS most commonly take the form of problem-based tasks (see page 44). Typically the vignette gives details of a current real-life situation and some background information. An example of a PALS is shown in Box 3.7.

There are a number of factors to consider in the design of vignettes for purposes of PALS (adapted from Norton, 2004).

- The scenario should link easily to recently studied syllabus-relevant theory.
- The scenario should be presented in a real-world context.
- The tasks should have just enough structure to guide students without discouraging independent thinking.
- The scenario and background should contain a number of cues to link into theory. For example, in Box 3.7 we are told that John is used to large amounts of coffee (cue for state-dependent forgetting) and that he has not seen the exam hall before (cue for context-dependent forgetting).
- The scenario should be inherently interesting so that thinking is stimulated.

Box 3.7

An example of a PALS suitable for post-16 teaching

Scenario: It is the start of John's first psychology AS exam. This is his first exam and he has never been in the exam hall before. In order to avoid needing the toilet during the exam he has not had his usual coffee that morning. He is feeling tired and rather sluggish. He turns over the paper and sees the first question, which concerns psychodynamic theory. Although the question looks straightforward John finds he cannot recall any of the material.

Background: John has had a traumatic year. His relationship with his parents has deteriorated to the point where he has left home and is staying with friends. He got behind on work earlier in the year and has recently been cramming, revising far into the night and keeping awake by drinking large amounts of coffee.

Tasks
1. Suggest how John's experience of forgetting can be explained in terms of cue dependency. Consider the role of both state and context cues.
2. Suggest a way in which repression might contribute to John's experience of forgetting.
3. Drawing on both theories of forgetting, what might John have done to avoid this experience?

Experiential learning

The term 'experiential learning' has been used very differently in different contexts. Here it is used in a broad sense to refer to any activities in which students have psychology, in its research or applied forms, conducted on them. This can range from playing the role of participants in professional research to introspective self-analysis.

Research participation

Psychology is a research-based discipline, and a straightforward way for students to experience some 'real' psychology first-hand is for them to take part in academic research as participants. Bowman and Waite (2003) studied the attitudes to participation in research of American college students. Students were offered the choice of writing a short paper or research participation as part of a research methods course. Those who opted to take part in a participant pool to be researched rated the research methods course more positively.

So what of the practicalities? Psychology teacher Craig Roberts has pioneered a model of research participation – the 'Psychology Day'. This involves setting aside a day and inviting local universities to submit details of current research projects for which post-16 students might prove suitable participants. The limiting factor that slows the progress of much research is the availability of participants; the opportunity to capture a few dozen participants in a day or half a day is often a heaven-sent opportunity for researchers! There should therefore be no shortage of researchers wanting to take part. In return for a steady supply of volunteer participants researchers are usually more than happy to give detailed debriefings about their studies.

Note that once a range of submissions has been received it is important to vet them for ethical issues. University ethics committees consider the balance of potential benefits and risks of research. Post-16 institutions have no such commitment to research, simply a responsibility for the welfare of students. We may therefore be rather stricter in drawing the lines about what is acceptable conduct in research. It is also worth involving students at this point to help consider what studies will provide them with an interesting experience. Once studies are approved it just remains to recruit volunteers for the studies.

Introspective tasks

There is a wide range of tasks that require students to introspect and relate psychological material to their own lives. There are of course serious ethical issues to consider here; some introspection tasks tread a fine line between teaching and therapy, to which students have not given informed consent and for which most teachers are not qualified. As a general rule steer clear of references to the more intimate and emotionally charged elements of students' own lives, for example parental relationships and mental health problems. It is also worth resisting the temptation to give students personality tests to aid introspection – the humble and omnipresent Eysenck Personality Inventory (EPI) may appear innocuous but in fact contains some very similar items to clinical tests like the Beck Depression Inventory. This can be very upsetting for students who have previously been assessed for depression.

There are, however, ways to use introspection as a teaching tool and stay on safer ground. In introducing social psychological studies that have involved testing both beliefs and behaviour, polls can be conducted, testing for example what proportion of students would obey Milgram's orders and shock Mr Wallace, or obey Dr Smith's orders to administer Astrofen were they to find themselves in Hofling *et al.*'s study. In teaching about flashbulb memories it is possible to pick a major event, such as the 9/11 attacks, and ask students to recall what they were doing when they heard the news and what peripheral details they can recall. These tasks do require introspection and by doing so help make psychological research and theory more relevant, but would not normally risk causing distress.

4. Making learning memorable: the role of information processing strategies

Historically there has been a tension between the constructivist ideal in which students learn actively and construct their own individual mental representations of topics, and the information-processing model that emphasises the virtues of teacher-organisation of material so that it can be made more memorable. Actually these visions are not irreconcilable; irrespective of what teaching strategies we use to cover post-16 syllabi, students will be assessed by means of exams. This requires that they are helped to organise and learn material, both at the point of delivery and during revision (Gage and Berliner, 1991). Moreover, the depth of processing and elaboration involved in constructivist tasks makes them perfectly compatible with information-processing principles.

Tools of organisation; advance organisers and revision checklists

Informing students of what is coming at the start of a lesson or topic can be of value in helping them organise the information they then go on to acquire. Ausubel (1968) has called this type of preparation an *advance organiser*. Advance organisers can take the form of anything that helps students recognise the place of each thing they go on to learn. They can take the form – *de rigueur* with Ofsted at the time of writing – of putting up aims/objectives of each lesson for students to refer back to as they go. There are however other ways of organising information in advance, for example at the start of a task and at the start of a topic. Three ways of organising material in advance are shown in Box 3.8. Note these are just examples and not intended to be definitive.

Note that these sorts of checklists – especially when structured by topic – are suitable for use as revision checklists. However, a substantial minority of students benefit significantly from having them at the beginning of topics. A meta-analysis of 135 studies of advance organisation of material (Luiten *et al.*, 1980) showed a small but consistent positive effect of their use, irrespective of age, level and subject. It is likely, though, that small average effects obscure large effects for particular students – experience suggests that some students benefit enormously from advance organisation.

Box 3.8

Three examples of advance organisation

1. **A lesson**

By the end of today's lesson you should be able to:

● Describe Milgram's classic study of obedience

● Outline some variations on the original procedure

● Know about ethical issues in research and consider the ethics of Milgram's procedures

● Evaluate Milgram's study.

2. **A task**

The write-up of this practical must be structured into the following sections:

● Abstract – a short summary of what you did and found

● Introduction – a mini-essay on relevant past research

● Hypothesis – a prediction of what you expected to find

● Method – how you went about the investigation

● Results – what you found in the investigation

● Discussion – a mini-essay on the implications of your findings

3. **A topic**

In clinical psychology you will need to be familiar with the following:

● Two ways of defining abnormality: statistical abnormality and deviation from social norms

● The DSM system of diagnosis

● Issues of reliability and validity in diagnosis

● The consequences of receiving a diagnosis

● Cultural issues in diagnosis

● The biomedical model of abnormality + one medical treatment

● The behavioural model + one behavioural therapy

● The cognitive model + one cognitive-behavioural therapy

● The psychodynamic model + one psychodynamic therapy

● The humanistic model + one humanistic therapy

● The social model + one social approach to treatment

● Two mental disorders: symptoms, and contributing biological, psychological and social factors.

The role of recall practice: tests and quizzes

One of the most robust effects in the literature of psychology teaching can be found in the benefits of testing students. Testing has a range of potential benefits for students. In cognitive terms it creates recall pathways, facilitating efficient recall under exam conditions. In motivational terms it provides an incentive to keep up with work and to keep material well organised. It thus encourages good study habits.

There are a number of variations in the way we can conduct tests. Leeming (2002) evaluated the 'exam-a-day' approach with four psychology classes at an American college. This involved administering a short test at the start of each lesson then moving on to the normal lesson format. As compared with controls the classes having the 'exam-a-day' had better retention, better student evaluations and better summative test results. The practical limitations of such regular testing include the additional preparation time and the total lost teaching time. The advantages lie in the expertise students gain in recall and the fact that they are well focused on psychology at the start of the normal lesson format.

An alternative to every-lesson testing is random administration of tests. An archival study by Sappington, Kinsey and Munasayac (2002) showed an association between grades and the use of random quizzes. This is supported by a study by Ruscio (2001), in which college students were administered random quizzes to assess their independent reading. Rates of reading were found to rise significantly!

Exam preparation: the role of metacognitive strategies

At A-level, preparation for formal assessment primarily involves learning to answer exam questions. Clearly one aspect of this is mastery of the necessary material and practising its recall. However there is a further dimension to exam preparation – learning to interpret and answer questions. Although there are dangers in what I call the utilitarian model of psychology teaching – constantly emphasising the exam preparation at the expense of fostering enthusiasm and developing transferable skills – we should not assume that students' knowledge and generic skills will necessarily translate into successful exam performance.

So what constitutes effective preparation for exams? Practice certainly, but there is a growing awareness that too much emphasis on simply drilling students with practice questions is ineffective, or at least provides a diminishing return. A more modern psychological understanding of effective exam preparation may be in terms of students' *metacognition*. This is a term we often hear nowadays in education, but it has been inconsistently used, leaving many teachers with a vague anxiety that they should but don't understand it! At its simplest, metacognition can be defined as the process of thinking about our own thinking. Larkin (2002) has teased this out a little further, providing a helpful definition as 'a form of cognition, a second or higher-level process. It involves both a knowledge of cognitive processing (how am I thinking about this?) and a conscious control and monitoring of that processing (would it be better if I thought about this differently?)' (2002: p. 65). The rationale behind much of the current interest in metacognition is that if students have a good metacognitive understanding of what and how they are studying they can better regulate their performance, for example in exams. Flavell (1985) identifies three types of knowledge we make use of in metacognition: personal knowledge, task knowledge and strategy knowledge. These can all be applied to exam preparation.

- **Personal knowledge:** knowledge about ourselves. In relation to exam preparation this might involve students being aware of their vulnerability to exam stress and their personal exam-skill strengths and weaknesses, for example essay writing, question interpretation and exam timing.
- **Task knowledge:** in terms of preparing students for exams this is particularly important. Students should be aware of the tasks they will face, for example analysing questions and planning answers.
- **Strategy knowledge:** this is related to task knowledge, referring to awareness of how to respond to the tasks they will face.

Box 3.9

Metacognitive strategies for exam preparation

- *Make sure students are fully aware of the assessment objectives and their significance*. This is an essential aspect of task knowledge and a prerequisite for any work done on question analysis.
- *Practise analysing injunctions*. Students frequently lose marks for describing rather than evaluating and (less often) vice versa. One way to tackle this is by exercises, which can be in whole-class or small groups in which students explicitly identify the assessment objectives questions are getting at.
- *Practise analysing question content*. Another way in which students lose marks is to misunderstand what content a question requires. One common reason for this is failing to read whole questions in the stress of the exam and responding to the first clause. This can be tackled by group exercises in which students practise breaking down questions.
- *Practise analysing and marking answers*. A useful exercise is for students to practise spotting AO1 and AO2 elements in longer answers. To vary this give some sample answers to AO2 questions where in some cases the answers are AO1 and in others AO2, and have them identify which answers would score.
- *Experiment with different formats for revision notes*. To develop personal knowledge let students see what format suits their information processing style. Note that learning style classifications do not have sufficient validity to use as the sole basis to advise students about revision notes.

Summary and conclusions

Although it would be very incautious to identify a best way of teaching psychology we can abstract from contemporary research a set of principles that can be said to reliably enhance learning. The constructivist paradigm emphasises the role of learning as an active and interactive process. We can make learning post-16 psychology an active process by means of enquiry-based, problem-based and multiple-perspective tasks. These can be performed individually and collaboratively. Collaboration adds a further dimension to learning, making use of on-task interactions to enhance the quality of student understanding. Jigsaw tasks are a useful way of speeding up collaborative learning, which can otherwise be a slow process. Peer tutoring, while requiring a degree of organisation, can be a highly effective way of providing students with valuable individual scaffolding.

There are of course other ways in which learning can be enhanced. Careful selection of psychological material and use of real-life material in the form of media stories and PALS can make psychology more relevant to the experiences of students. Students can also experience some 'real' psychology by participation in professional research – this is easier to organise than we might suspect. Finally, good teaching of a topic can be enhanced from the student perspective by the use of information-processing strategies to make the material more memorable. Advance organisers are one helpful approach. The use of quizzes has been found reliably to improve recall under exam conditions, and metacognitive strategies can further help by ensuring that students do not lose marks by misinterpreting or wrongly answering exam questions.

Self-assessment questions

1. What are the features of an authentic constructivist task? Compare enquiry-based, problem-based and multiple-perspective tasks as approaches to making learning an active process.

2. Outline the strengths and limitations of collaborative learning.

3. How can academic psychology be made relevant to the lives of post-16 students?

4. What is a PALS? Design a PALS for use in teaching an area of your choice.

5. Summarise the ways in which you would make sure students are prepared for exams.

Further reading

•••••• Cook, J.L. (2005) *Constructing knowledge: the value of teaching from multiple perspectives*. Paper delivered at the NITOP annual conference.

•••••• Jarvis, M. (2005) *The Psychology of Effective Learning and Teaching*. Nelson Thornes, Cheltenham.

•••••• Leeming, F.C. (2002) The exam-a-day procedure improves performance in psychology classes. *Teaching of Psychology*, **29**, 210–212.

•••••• Norton, L. (2004) *Psychology Applied Learning Scenarios (PALS): A Practical Introduction to Problem-based Learning Using Vignettes for Psychology Lecturers.* LTSN, York.

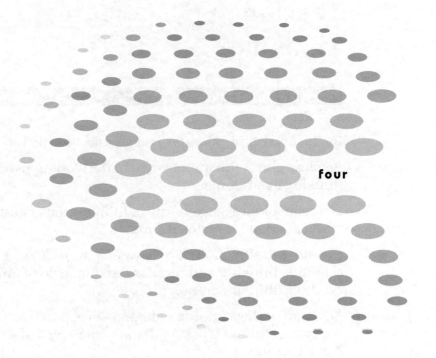

four

Teaching
psychological
thinking

Teaching psychological thinking

By the end of this chapter you should be able to:

• Be clear about the importance of developing psychological thinking in students.

• Describe Bloom's taxonomy of thinking skills and understand its application in assessing A-levels.

• Consider the relationship between psychological thinking and scientific thinking and discuss the dual role of analytic and synthetic thinking in psychology.

• Apply an understanding of higher-level psychological thinking to assessing student work, with particular regard to the work of Peter Facione.

• Understand how to use a range of activities to develop higher-level thinking in the psychology classroom, including the use of elaborated evaluation, repertory grids and evaluation toolkits.

• Outline, apply and evaluate Sternberg's triarchic model of psychology teaching.

It is widely acknowledged that psychology is as much a way of thinking as it is a collection of knowledge, theory and research. What distinguishes a good psychologist or psychology student is not merely how much they know but how deeply and effectively they can think about the subject. As B.F. Skinner reportedly remarked, education is 'what is left when you've forgotten what you've learnt' (cited in Swansea University student bar). Much of what the successful psychology student takes away from the subject is in the form of thinking skills. This much is truism, but exactly what sort of thinking are we talking about? How are thinking skills tied into the post-16 psychology curriculum and what strategies can psychology teachers use to assess and develop them? The aim of this chapter is to answer these rather lofty questions in terms of practical classroom solutions.

What are thinking skills and why are they important?

Advantages conferred by advanced thinking

In education there has generally been a significant shift over the last decade towards making the development of thinking skills a priority. This is widely believed to be important for both the individual and society. On the societal level thinking skills are likely to become increasingly important in tackling world problems. Philosopher Richard Paul (1993) refers to the 'deep-seated problems of environmental damage, human relations, overpopulation, rising expectations, diminishing resources, global competition, personal goals and ideological conflict' (1993: p. 1) that face future generations and will require imaginative and critical thought to tackle.

On the level of the individual, Wilson (2000) suggests that a broad range of higher thinking skills is beneficial on the grounds of cognitive efficiency. In the current climate in which the volume of information we are required to process is ever increasing, we simply cannot store sufficient information to respond to every situation without being able to transfer skills from one situation to another. This can be very important at post-16 level. Consider the cognitive load for an A-level student preparing for an exam in which he or she can be asked to evaluate one or more of dozens of empirical studies. To learn a toolkit of evaluation skills involves higher-level thinking and so is initially a difficult task. However, once achieved the student can go into the exam without having had to learn separate evaluation points for a large number of studies. In cognitive terms this is a much more efficient strategy.

There are also more distal advantages to enhancing students' thinking skills. Higher-level thinking skills are important when we come to consider preparing students for study at HE level. There is a body of research showing that students with good higher level thinking skills do better in psychology degrees. In one recent American study Williams *et al.* (2003) assessed 149 psychology undergraduates for thinking skills and found that critical thinking as assessed at the start of the course correlated ($r = 0.41$) with exam performance, accounting for 26% of the variance in results. Although thinking skills were found to improve during the course this still shows that the starting point for thinking skills at entry to HE is significant.

In a fascinating account of a workshop for HE teachers on post-16 psychology run as part of the *Writing in the Disciplines* project (see www.learndev.qmul.ac.uk for details), Tombs (2004) reported that HE teachers tended to be surprised and impressed by the volume of information covered at A-level but critical of the superficial evaluation skills usually developed and the lack of time allowed by the specifications for students to develop a sophisticated mental representation of psychological material.

This is an extremely important point; as the awarding bodies face allegations of 'dumbing down' (see Chapter 2 for a discussion) it becomes increasingly difficult politically for those responsible for curriculum development to develop a less content-laden syllabus that better lends itself to the development of advanced thinking skills. It thus falls to the psychology teacher to use effective strategies to promote higher-level thinking.

Bloom's taxonomy and psychology A-level

The term 'thinking skills' is not a clear one, and some commentators have questioned whether we are technically correct to think of cognitive processes as skills that can be learned in the same way as motor skills (Wilson, 2000). Helpfully, Wilson has redefined the central question facing teachers and researchers as 'can [students] be taught to think more effectively?' (2000: p. 2). When we speak of 'thinking' in this context we are not referring so much to the stream of consciousness that describes our moment-by-moment experience of thinking, but rather a set of *higher order* mental processes. There have been a number of attempts to classify such higher order processes. Particularly influential at A-level has been the taxonomy developed by Bloom *et al.* (1956). This is shown in Figure 4.1.

To Bloom and colleagues there were six levels of thinking, which we can think as the cognitive goals of education. These were seen as an ascending

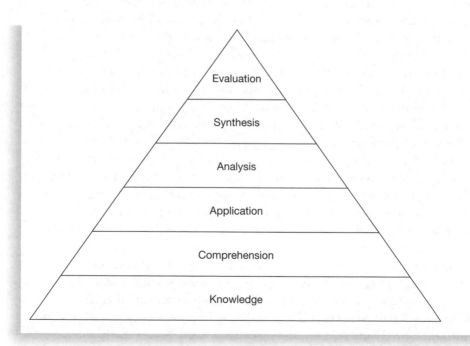

Figure 4.1 **Bloom's taxonomy**

hierarchy, the most basic being knowledge and the highest evaluation. Bloom *et al.*'s approach has been enormously influential in curriculum design and assessment. Consider the assessment objectives adopted by the awarding bodies for post-2000 A- and AS-levels. These are framed in terms of assessment objectives, one representing Bloom *et al.*'s basic levels of knowledge and understanding and another representing their higher goals. Take the specifications for psychology A-level (Edexcel, AQA and OCR, 2000). AO1 is defined as knowledge and understanding. AO2, representing higher thinking skills, is worded thus: 'analysis, evaluation and application' (OCR), 'application of knowledge and understanding, analysis, synthesis and evaluation' (Edexcel) and 'analyse and evaluate' (AQA) (see also Chapter 2 for discussion of assessment objectives). In keeping with the belief that analysis, synthesis and evaluation represent more advanced levels of thinking, the proportion of marks available for AO2 is greater at A2 than AS level.

- *Knowledge*: knowledge of a subject is shown by identifying, defining and outlining psychological ideas, theories, studies and applications. This is the simplest form of thinking to teach and assess, and does not require higher-level thinking.
- *Understanding*: understanding is demonstrated by rephrasing, clarifying, explaining and drawing conclusions from psychological material.
- *Application*: application takes place when an understanding of theory and/or research is used to explain a scenario such as a real-life situation.
- *Analysis*: analysis involves going beyond the obvious information, breaking down a concept or situation in order to better understand it. This might for example involve suggesting where an idea came from or what factors might underlie a situation.
- *Synthesis*: This is roughly equivalent to the concept of creativity. Synthesis takes place when we put ideas together in an imaginative way, perhaps designing a new programme or improving an existing theory or research method.
- *Evaluation*: This is roughly equivalent to the concept of critical thinking. Evaluation is demonstrated when we make judgements about an idea, theory, study or practice. How to evaluate theories and studies is addressed in detail on page 72.

Fisher (1995, adapted for A-level by Jarvis, 2005) has offered a set of injunctions designed to cue students to employ each of Bloom's thinking skills. These may be of use in both class discussions and written tasks. These are shown in Table 4.1.

Table 4.1 **Thinking process cues**

Level	Thinking skill	Cues for classroom exercises
1	Knowledge	Describe, outline, recall, repeat, define, identify, which, where, who, what?
2	Understanding	Summarise, rephrase, explain, conclude, relate, interpret, why?
3	Application	Demonstrate, apply, use to solve, use to explain.
4	Analysis	Identify the causes, compare, reasons, problems, solutions, consequences.
5	Synthesis	Develop, improve, design, create, put together, tell a story.
6	Evaluation	Judge, criticise, evaluate the success, practical value, coherence, validity.

Psychological thinking and scientific thinking

In its early days psychology struggled for recognition as a science, and some of the early movements in psychology, most obviously behaviourism, based their credibility on their visible scientific credentials. The situation has changed and the question is no longer so much 'is psychology a science?' but rather 'given psychology's diversity and that it is classified as a science, what is science itself?' A full discussion of the relationship between psychology and science is not within the scope of this book, but it has clear implications for defining what we mean by psychological thinking. In other words, is psychological thinking the same as scientific thinking? According to McGhee (2001) the answer is a resounding 'no'. A good psychologist must be able to think like a scientist but also on occasion like an anthropologist, a historian, a philosopher and a therapist. This is a highly challenging notion for psychology teachers at both post-16 and degree level who (necessarily) spend considerable time inculcating in students an understanding of the scientific method. However, although we place considerable value on psychology as a science, even at introductory levels we *do* teach and value other ways of thinking, albeit often implicitly.

One way to understand the range of thinking that we might call 'psychological' is with reference to the distinction (Sternberg, 1997; McGhee 2001) between analytic and synthetic modes of thinking. In this context the terms 'analysis' and 'synthesis' are used rather more broadly than in Bloom's model. *Analytic* thinking is logical, based on drawing inferences from available data. By contrast *synthetic* thinking is free flowing and imaginative. We think analytically when we apply rules to decide the truth or falsity of an explanation, when we statistically analyse data and when we design an experiment to eliminate the influence of all independent variables bar the one we are interested in. This is very much traditional scientific thinking and many psychologists think of it as the correct way to think about psychology. However, without a degree of synthetic thinking sciences never make great leaps. As McGhee puts it: 'It is the imaginative leaps carried out by

Copernicus, Albert Einstein and Stephen Hawking that set them apart from their merely excellent peers.' Whenever we generate a new hypothesis to test a theory, use an analogy to make a model (such as the *multistore* model) accessible, or apply a psychological theory or idea to understanding a new situation, we are thinking synthetically. But what does this scientific philosophy have to do with classroom teaching? The answer is that being able to appreciate both analytic and synthetic thinking allows students to think more widely when looking for the commentary and evaluation that comprise AO2 marks. This is put into practice in designing thinking skills toolkits (see page 72) and is reflected in the type of sequenced learning activities that follow from Sternberg's triarchic model of psychology teaching (see page 78).

Analysing thinking skills

It can be instructive to teachers and students to be aware of the extent to which students are using higher-level thinking. Advanced thinking skills can be assessed by means of psychometric tests, such as the California Critical Thinking Dispositions Inventory (CCTDI), shown in Box 4.1. Note that the term 'critical thinking' is used here in a broad sense to mean higher-level thinking. In other contexts it is used more narrowly to mean evaluation.

However, most psychology teachers are not qualified to administer psychometric tests for diagnostic purposes (using them for demonstration and research purposes are greyer areas). This requires the British Psychological Society's *Statement and Certificate of Competence in Educational Testing*. Moreover, if anything students are already over-assessed and at risk of labelling effects. An alternative is to assess existing written work. The simplest

67

Box 4.1

The CCTDI

This has 75 items, measuring seven subscales of critical thinking: truth seeking, open mindedness, analyticity, systematicity, self-confidence, inquisitiveness and maturity. Answers are by means of a six-point Likert scale (strongly agree to strongly disagree).

Examples of items include the following:
- Studying new things all my life would be wonderful   (assesses inquisitiveness)
- It is impossible to know what standards to apply to most questions   (assesses analyticity)
- I believe what I want to believe   (assesses open-mindedness)

Source: Facione (1995)

Box 4.2

The Holistic Critical Thinking Rubric

4 Consistently does all or almost all of the following:
- Accurately interprets evidence, statements, graphics, questions, etc.
- Identifies the salient arguments (reasons and claims) pro and con.
- Thoughtfully analyses and evaluates major alternative points of view.
- Draws warranted, judicious, non-fallacious conclusions.
- Justifies key results and procedures, explains assumptions and reasons.
- Fair-mindedly follows where evidence and reasons lead.

3 Does most or many of the following:
- Accurately interprets evidence, statements, graphics, questions, etc.
- Identifies relevant arguments (reasons and claims) pro and con.
- Offers analyses and evaluations of obvious alternative points of view.
- Draws warranted, non-fallacious conclusions.
- Justifies some results or procedures, explains reasons.
- Fair-mindedly follows where evidence and reasons lead.

2 Does most or many of the following:
- Misinterprets evidence, statements, graphics, questions, etc.
- Fails to identify strong, relevant counter-arguments.
- Ignores or superficially evaluates obvious alternative points of view.
- Draws unwarranted or fallacious conclusions.
- Justifies few results or procedures, seldom explains reasons.
- Regardless of the evidence or reasons, maintains or defends views based on self-interest or preconceptions.

1 Consistently does all or almost all of the following:
- Offers biased interpretations of evidence, statements, graphics, questions, information, or the points of view of others.
- Fails to identify or hastily dismisses strong, relevant counter-arguments.
- Ignores or superficially evaluates obvious alternative points of view.
- Argues using fallacious or irrelevant reasons, and unwarranted claims.
- Does not justify results or procedures, nor explain reasons.
- Regardless of the evidence or reasons, maintains or defends views based on self-interest or preconceptions.
- Exhibits close-mindedness or hostility to reason.

Source: P. A. Facione and N.C. Facione (1994).
Holistic Critical Thinking Scoring Rubric (HCTSR).
California Academic Press: Millbrae CA 94030

69

way of doing this is by means of published mark schemes from the awarding bodies. However these tend to give at least limited credit to brief or formulaic evaluation and analysis (Tombs, 2004). This means that students can learn to survive the exam system without developing the thinking skills that would gain them the top marks and be transferable to other contexts. A way around this is to use Facione and Facione's (1994) *Holistic Critical Thinking Scoring Rubric*. This is shown in Box 4.2.

Because it is not tied to any particular mark scheme, Facione's rubric may provide a better general tool for assessing the sophistication of thinking in student written work. It can be used to directly show students what they are doing correctly and incorrectly. This is often not easy by means of published mark schemes. Remember that these are constructed primarily to achieve acceptable levels of reliability and validity in the marking process, *not* to give students formative feedback. For more information about Facione's rubric see http://www.insightassessment.com/pdf_files/rubric.pdf.

Strategies to develop thinking skills

All psychology teachers working at all levels constantly use multiple strategies to encourage students to think beyond Bloom's basic levels of knowledge and understanding. Whenever we pose a question to a group, praise a creative response to psychological material or discuss the strengths and weaknesses of a study, theory or method we are promoting higher-level thinking. The strategies discussed in this chapter are in the form of tasks and prompts specifically designed to push students to think in advanced ways to which they might not be accustomed. In an influential report Carol McGuinness (1999) concluded that, irrespective of different theoretical bases, alternative approaches to developing thinking skills share the ultimate goal of bringing about qualitative change in the type of thinking of which learners are capable. In terms of their rationale for doing this they tend to share a number of core concepts:

- Learners are active creators of their knowledge, thus it is necessary for learners to seek meaning and impose structure on learning material as opposed to passively absorb it. Development of thinking skills is thus closely related to the constructivist tradition (discussed in Chapter 3).
- A classroom focus on thinking skills is beneficial because it leads to development of activities that support active information processing strategies.
- Learners can be and need to be taught the skills of higher-level thinking.
- Development of thinking skills requires a taxonomy of skills to be developed or selected. That of Bloom *et al.* (1956) is an example of a thinking skills taxonomy.

- Effective teaching of thinking skills involves developing non-routine tasks, which require higher level thinking to complete successfully.
- Learners need to develop better awareness of their own thought processes and to reflect consciously on them. This type of awareness is called *metacognition*.
- There are important social aspects to learning, and learners pick up thinking strategies from each other and from teachers. Social interaction should thus be oriented towards a thinking skills perspective.
- Thinking takes place in a cultural context, and the culture of the learning environment must reflect the value placed on thinking skills. Thus questioning and challenge should be encouraged.
- Teachers and institutions can benefit from improvements in thinking skills as well as individual learners.

AO2 elaboration exercises

Assessment Objective 2 is meant to assess and so encourage the development of higher level thinking skills. However, AO2 and higher-level thinking are not synonymous. Whilst to gain high AO2 marks it is probably necessary to think deeply about psychological material, some marks can be gained by brief, superficial and formularised comments. One way to encourage psychological thinking that directly impacts both proximally on AO2 marks and distally on thinking skills is to elaborate AO2 answers. A useful strategy to begin this process can be to deny students the tools for producing formulaic answers. Thus the term 'ecological validity', which is liberally and sometimes indiscriminately scattered throughout A-level answers without elaboration, may be best not introduced until students have a thorough understanding of the significance of the environment in which studies are conducted.

A three-stage strategy to elaborate AO2 answers

1. The initial exercise is to have students analyse the differences between examples of superficial and elaborate evaluation. This both puts their analytical skills to work and provides a template of what an elaborated AO2 answer looks like. It is heavily cued by the use of specific questions. If we think in terms of evaluation being picked up across a zone of proximal development these cues provide the scaffolding. An example is shown in Box 4.3.
2. The next stage is for students to take examples of superficial evaluation and develop them into an elaborated form. This is a more autonomous task, however the stimulus of the superficial evaluation provides a degree of scaffolding. An example is shown in Box 4.4.

Box 4.3

An example of analysing the differences between superficial and elaborated evaluation

Question: Discuss the ethical issues associated with Milgram's obedience experiment.

Answer one.
Milgram was unethical. He lied to participants and told them they couldn't leave. It also lacked ecological validity.

Answer two.
Milgram's work took place before the development of ethical guidelines so it is questionable whether he should be judged retrospectively by these standards. Milgram misled participants about the point of the experiment and that Mr Wallace was badly hurt or dead. This of course was necessary for the experiment to work. He also caused them distress and, most seriously, he denied them the right to withdraw. On the other hand he debriefed them and followed them up to make sure they were all right.

Questions
1. Both answers are evaluations of Milgram. Which answer focuses better on the issue of ethics?
2. How does answer two set Milgram's work in context?
3. What blunt statements are made in answer one make that could be expanded upon?
4. Answer two is more balanced. In what ways does it put across both sides of the argument?
5. Give one mark for each fully made point to each answer. As marker, what would you give each answer?

Box 4.4

An example of an elaboration task

For each of the following superficial elaboration points, develop a more elaborated evaluation.

Superficial evaluation	Elaborated evaluation
1 Milgram lacked ecological validity	
2 Milgram's research was important	
3 Milgram's study was unethical	

3. The third stage is to put the understanding and practice developed in the first two stages into practice by administering AO2 questions. The twist in the plot at this point is to *not* give mark allocations with the questions. The task is for students to write as much as they can without distracting thoughts about whether they have reached the maximum mark.

Evaluation toolkits

Like the three-stage model of extended elaboration, thinking toolkits owe much to Vygotskian theory. Vygotsky saw the development of advanced thinking as a process of internalisation of external dialogue to form mental tools. From this perspective achievement of higher-level thinking in students depends on establishing such dialogue. The rationale for evaluation toolkits is that they provide the basis of such dialogue, which can be internalised to form a set of mental tools for critical thinking. Thinking for a moment in terms of cultural deprivation, this may serve as a leveller, allowing students who have not had the previous experience of such dialogues to compete on a more level playing field with those who, as a function of their social background or educational experiences, are used to thinking in critical terms.

Based on the distinction between analytic and synthetic thinking, McGhee (2001) has offered a set of toolkits for thinking in both ways about psychological theory and research. Thinking analytically involves consideration of ethics, validity, hypothesis derivation, experimental, control etc. Thinking synthetically involves application to real-world situations, identifying unexpected trends in data and consideration of historical and cultural context.

McGhee's toolkits are well worth reading in full, however they are conceptually advanced and aimed at higher-level study. The following toolkits are offered to guide evaluation in post-16 psychology. Box 4.5 shows a toolkit for evaluating studies and Box 4.6 a toolkit for evaluating theories. Both of these include elements of analytic and synthetic thinking, although there is probably little benefit in burdening students with the distinction. The art to using these toolkits* is to remember that none of these issues will apply equally to every theory and study, and to match the salient issue to the material being evaluated. Note also that there is a minimum of technical language in these versions. This is because students with limited understanding tend to use terms like 'ecological validity', 'face validity' and 'heuristic value' glibly and without elaboration. Withholding these terms until students have mastered their meaning forces them to explain what they mean.

---

* Feel free to copy and use these proformas but please credit me in any publications.

Box 4.5

Evaluation of study toolkit

Issue	Cue questions	Student elaborated response
1 Ethics	What ethical issues are raised? e.g. harm, distress, consent, deceit, withdrawal, privacy. Does the importance of results outweigh the cost to participants?	
2 Social sensitivity	Is the whole topic taboo? Do results justify discrimination? Do results suggest something unpleasant about human nature?	
3 Sample	Is overall sample size large? Is the sample in each condition large? Is the sample representative?	
4 Environment	Is the environment controlled? Is the environment natural?	
5 Design	Is the design particularly clever? Is there a flaw in the design? Are there inevitable limitations to this type of design, e.g. non-matched groups in natural experiments?	
6 Measures	Are measures of DVs standard or constructed for this study? Do measures seem to be reliable? Do measures seem to be valid?	
7 Theoretical importance	Is the study significant because it provides evidence for or against an important theory?	
8 Practical applications	Does the study have important real-world applications?	

73

Box 4.6

Evaluation of theory toolkit

	Issue	Cue questions	Student elaborated response
1	Credibility and simplicity	Does the theory make sense? Does it appear to explain a psychological phenomenon? Is there a more obvious explanation that could explain the same data?	
2	Origins	Is the theory built on solid foundations such as good quality research? Is it founded on limited evidence or plucked out of thin air?	
3	Testability	Can any aspects of the theory be tested by psychological studies? Are there parts of the theory that are hard to test by means of psychological studies?	
4	Supporting evidence	Are there studies that support all or part of the theory?	
5	Conflicting evidence	Are there studies that suggest the theory is incorrect?	
6	Completeness	Is there anything important that the theory cannot explain?	
7	Value to psychology	Does the theory help us understand or think about something?	
8	Value to society	Does the theory have practical applications in the real world?	

Repertory techniques

Repertory techniques (Kelly, 1955) are an alternative approach to providing the cues to facilitate higher-level thinking. These come in various formats but share the purpose of making concrete and visible a range of perceptions about an aspect of the world, most commonly a set of interpersonal relationships. These perceptions are called *personal constructs*. Mayo (2004) has applied the repertory grid technique to helping psychology students analyse psychological theories. The same approach can be used for theory and lends itself to both analysis and evaluation of psychological material. Repertory grids are particularly useful for comparing alternative theories and studies. Examples are shown in Box 4.7.

Box 4.7

Use of repertory grids for developing higher-level thinking

1. Evaluation of theories of memory

Theories of memory	Credibility/ face validity	Supporting evidence	Conflicting evidence	Complete explanation	Practical applications
Multistore model	✓	✓	✓	✗	✓
Levels of processing	✓	✓	✗	✗	✓
Working memory	✓	✓	✗	✗	✓

2. Evaluation of studies of obedience

Studies of obedience	Ethical	Socially sensitive	Representative sample	Natural environment	Control	Valid measures	Practical applications
Milgram	✗	✓	✗	✗	✓	✓	✓
Hofling	✓	✓	✗	✓	✓	✓	✓
Tarnow	✓	✓	✓	✓	✗	✗	✓

A limitation of using the traditional binary response format (i.e. yes/no) in repertory grids is that it may encourage unelaborated answers. It can still be a useful starting point; however, as Mayo suggests, a better response format is a seven-point semantic differential-type rating scale. For example Milgram's study would be evaluated as follows:

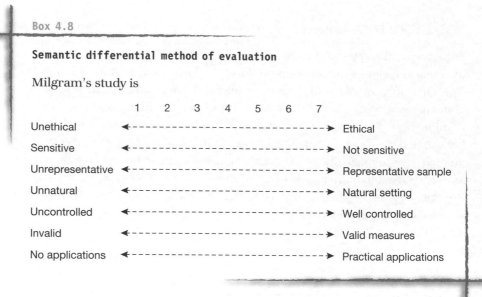

Box 4.8

Semantic differential method of evaluation

Milgram's study is

	1	2	3	4	5	6	7	
Unethical	←- -→							Ethical
Sensitive	←- -→							Not sensitive
Unrepresentative	←- -→							Representative sample
Unnatural	←- -→							Natural setting
Uncontrolled	←- -→							Well controlled
Invalid	←- -→							Valid measures
No applications	←- -→							Practical applications

One of the strengths of repertory techniques, whether in binary form for comparison or in semantic differential form for more in-depth analytical thinking about particular theories or studies, is their potential for use in co-operative learning and for stimulating whole-class discussion. Mayo reports that students surveyed on the use of repertory techniques were enthusiastic and that they were associated with improved test results.

Peer evaluation

All the above techniques can be carried out individually or in co-operative groups. However there are also approaches to developing higher-level thinking that aim specifically to make use of peer interaction. One such approach is *peer evaluation*, i.e. students critically evaluating each other's work. Anderson *et al.* (2001) used a peer-based strategy to teach the importance of evidence to Health and Social Care students at an FE college. Students were given ten didactic lessons about the importance of evidence then the task of designing a health or social care institution or a health promotion campaign. They were then required to use their critical thinking to critique designs, initially imaginary examples then each other's. Content analysis of later projects showed an increased awareness of the importance of evidence.

Peer evaluation can be applied to several aspects of post-16 psychology. Coursework designs are one example of where the approach used by Anderson and colleagues (above) can be applied to A-level. Toolkits and repertory techniques can be used to provide structure for this type of exercise. Students can also learn to mark past exam questions and give each other feedback. An obvious issue with this type of peer assessment is the validity of the feedback given by inexperienced student markers. In a meta-analysis of studies of peer assessment Falchikov and Goldfinch (2000) found good levels of agreement between teachers and students at undergraduate level, however it is unclear to what extent this is true at post-16 level. Falchikov and Goldfinch offer the following advice about peer assessment:

- Peer and teacher assessments of student work agree more closely when global measures are used rather than attempts to break down the mark to components.
- Peer and teacher assessment tend to agree more when the student work concerns theory and research as opposed to practical applications of psychology.
- Peer and teacher assessments tend to agree more where good quality work is being evaluated.

Metacognitive prompts

The techniques reviewed thus far are essentially student centred. However there is also a place for whole-class teaching in developing thinking skills. One way of thinking about effective development of thinking during whole-class teaching is in terms of metacognitive prompts. Metacognition is discussed in detail in Chapter 3. Briefly, it refers to our cognitive awareness of our own mental processes. This awareness relies on three types of information: self-knowledge, task knowledge and strategy knowledge. There is a growing consensus among education experts that one of the keys to developing higher-level thinking is to encourage metacognition. The terms we use to give feedback to students can be used to provide cues for metacognitive knowledge. Examples are shown in Table 4.2.

Table 4.2 **Teacher prompts to elicit metacognition**

Metacognitive knowledge	Type of prompt	Example
Self	Focus on abilities	'You really enjoy this sort of thinking, don't you?'
	Focus on learning style	'Does seeing it in a table like that make it easier?'
	Focus on learning strategy	'What do you do when you get homework like this?'
	Focus on motivational style	'Do you find it easier in small chunks like this?'
Task	Focus on assessment criteria	'What am I looking for when I mark this?'
	Comparison with other tasks	'What did you find last time we did this?'
	Focus on critical thinking	'Can you see anything dodgy about that?'
	Focus on creative thinking	'What can we do about that?'
Strategy	Focus on thinking	'Put your thinking cap on for a moment.'
	Focus on planning	'What's the first thing we have to do?'
	Focus on checking	'Good. Now look back at what you've done.'

Sternberg's triarchic model of psychology teaching

In recent years there has been a growing awareness of the broad range of human mental abilities and a realisation that traditional teaching methods may not always make the best use of these. In response an enormous number of theories and techniques have emerged. Many of these theories have no empirical basis and many techniques are based on fundamental misunderstandings of respectable theory. One approach that stands out is Robert Sternberg's triarchic model of teaching. This was developed specifically as a way of teaching introductory psychology, although it has now been successfully employed in a range of subjects and age groups (Grigorenko *et al.*, 2002). The triarchic model seeks to maximise learning by means of employing three modes of thinking: analytic, synthetic and practical.

- Analytic: to Sternberg this is synonymous with critical thinking and involves breaking down a theory or study in order to identify its strengths and limitations.
- Synthetic: this is used in the same way as in other systems to mean creative thinking.
- Practical: this refers to the application of psychological theory or research to a real-world situation.

The rationale behind triarchic teaching is that students both think triarchically to learn and learn to think triarchically. In other words, by constructing lessons or sets of lessons that involve thinking in these three modes we can both aid learning *and* develop higher-level thinking skills. From this starting point we can put together lessons and schemes of work that contain a balance between tasks using each of these modes of thinking. Table 4.3 shows a set of cues for tasks that make use of each of the three modes. Box 4.9 shows three examples of how tasks requiring analytic, synthetic and practical thinking can be sequenced in a lesson. Note that in each case the tasks are in different order. There is no requirement in the triarchic model for analytic thinking to precede synthetic, etc.

Table 4.3 **Cues for analytic, synthetic and practical thinking tasks**

Mode of thinking	Examples of cues
Analytic	Assess, critique, criticise, evaluate, judge, analyse, argue for and against, question the evidence for, defend, debate, compare the contributions of.
Synthetic	Create, design, imagine, combine, put together, formulate a hypothesis.
Practical	Apply, use, implement, put into practice, demonstrate, explain using theory.

Adapted from Sternberg (1999)

Box 4.9

Three examples of task sequences based on triarchic theory

1: The debate over day care
- Explain using attachment theory how long hours in day care in early infancy might have negative effects on an infant's development (requires practical thinking).
- Assess the strength of the evidence that suggests that day care can have negative effects on infant development (requires analytic thinking).
- Design a leaflet offering advice to parents considering using day care (requires synthetic thinking).

2: Comparing psychoanalysis and cognitive-behavioural therapy (CBT)
- Compare the evidence for the effectiveness of analysis and CBT (requires analytic thinking).
- Put together some principles of psychoanalysis and CBT and come up with your own therapy (requires synthetic thinking).
- Bernard has come to therapy seeking help for his lack of confidence in meeting women. Use the principles of psychoanalysis and CBT to explain why he might have this problem and what can be done to help him (requires practical thinking).

3: Eyewitness testimony (EWT)
- Based on your knowledge of past studies, design your own study of eyewitness testimony that we can carry out in class (requires synthetic thinking).
- Explain using theories of memory and forgetting why EWT might be inaccurate (requires practical thinking).
- Assess the usefulness of eyewitness testimony as a source of evidence in the classroom (requires analytic thinking).

There is a small but respectable body of research to suggest that the triarchic approach is an effective approach to lesson planning. Sternberg and Clinkenbeard (1995) assessed 199 American college students for their preferences for critical, creative and practical thinking, and designed a course in introductory psychology that either corresponded or failed to correspond to these preferences. When assessed, students whose learning activities had been congruent with their preferences did significantly better, supporting the idea – central to triarchic theory – that individuals have strengths and weaknesses across the three domains. Sternberg *et al.* (1998) went on to compare a triarchic model of teaching with a traditional memory-based model of teaching and a critical thinking model, which focused on critical evaluation of material without creative or practical tasks. 141 American high school children were taught introductory psychology at a university summer school in three groups. One was memory-based, emphasising information processing strategies for learning psychological material. The second was critical thinking-based and the third was taught triarchically. Assessments showed that the triarchic group did best, followed by the critical thinking group and finally the memory-based group.

Summary and conclusions

It is now widely acknowledged that developing thinking skills is an important aspect of education and that the discipline of psychology requires the development of particular modes of thinking. The A-level curriculum is based on Bloom's taxonomy of basic and higher thinking skills, marked as AO1 and AO2. A common criticism of post-16 teaching from both HE teachers and A-level examiners is that there is a tendency for students to learn oversimple and formulaic strategies for gaining AO2 marks, often missing opportunities to develop genuine higher-level thinking abilities.

An important distinction in understanding psychological thinking is between analytic and synthetic modes of thinking. There are a number of strategies that can be used to develop analytic and synthetic thinking. This is likely to benefit students both in their post-16 achievements and in more advanced study. Such methods include AO2 evaluation, the use of evaluation toolkits and repertory techniques and peer evaluation. Sternberg has put forward a model of psychology teaching based on sequencing tasks of analytic, synthetic and practical thinking. The evidence base for these strategies is small but respectable. It does seem then that it is possible to develop higher level thinking in psychology students, but that it probably requires going beyond traditional teaching methods.

Self-assessment questions

1. Why are thinking skills important?

2. Explain the relationship between Bloom's taxonomy and A-level assessment objectives.

3. To what extent is psychological thinking scientific thinking?

4. Compare two classroom exercises that might be used to enhance critical thinking skills.

5. Describe and evaluate the triarchic model of psychology teaching.

Further reading

•••••◐ Facione, P.A. (1990) *Critical Thinking: A Statement of Expert Consensus for Purposes of Education Assessment and Instruction.* California Academic Press, Milbrae.

•••••◐ McGhee, P. (2001) *Thinking Psychologically.* Palgrave, Basingstoke.

•••••◐ http://www.patrickmcghee.co.uk

•••••◐ Sternberg, R.J., Torff, B. and Grigorenko, E.L. (1998) Teaching triarchically improves school achievement. *Journal of Educational Psychology*, **90**, 1–11.

•••••◐ Tombs, S. (2004) Writing, arguing and evaluation – the perspective from Higher Education. *Psychology Teaching*, Summer 2004, 36–38.

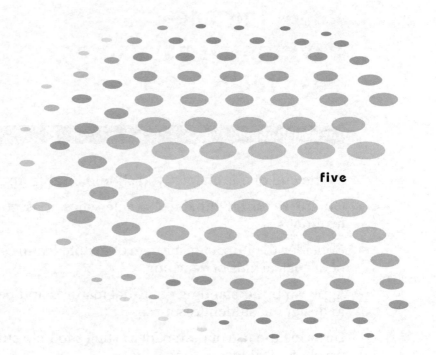

five

Choosing and developing psychology resources

Choosing and developing psychology resources

learning objectives

By the end of this chapter you should be able to:

- Outline research into the characteristics of psychology textbooks.

- Consider the impact of a range of textual features and pedagogical aids on learning.

- Apply an understanding of textual features and pedagogical aids to designing student resources.

- Describe the use of newspaper articles to help students apply psychological theory to real life.

- Discuss the use of popular culture to illustrate and demonstrate psychology with particular regard to the portrayal of mental disorder in film and the deconstruction of popular lyrics.

- Understand the benefits of using a range of formats for assessment materials.

All psychology teachers use a range of resources, produced both commercially and in-house, in order to put across psychological information. These include published textbooks and videos, as well as home-grown handouts and worksheets. They also include a range of resources intended for other purposes but imaginatively adapted for teaching. The aim of this chapter is to help teachers better understand some of the criteria by which existing resources can be evaluated and new ones developed. We are talking here of resources in conventional formats. Chapter 6 deals separately with on-line and software resources.

Psychology textbooks

For every post-16 psychology syllabus there is a choice of textbooks available. It would be inappropriate for several reasons to pick apart particular books or to make recommendations, although in Appendix I there is a list of publishers currently specialising in post-16 psychology. Perhaps the most basic question we can ask about psychology texts is: what are they like? There is a research tradition in the USA of content-analysing and comparing textbooks. This has been supplemented in the UK by a tradition of more critical qualitative research seeking to identify more subtle dimensions of content such as bias.

The sameness hypothesis

A popular stereotype of psychology texts, especially those produced in the USA, is that they are all pretty much the same. Actually research has shown that this apparent similarity is largely a product of similarity in chapter structures. This has always been the case in the USA where general academic psychology textbooks are most commonly structured around the standard first year undergraduate course (Psych 101). This similarity has increased in the UK in the last five years in which time there has been a move for books aimed specifically at the post-16 market to follow the structure of A-level specifications.

When Jackson *et al.* (2000) reviewed 41 American general introductory psychology texts they found that 39 followed an almost identical structure. However, this says little about the coverage within those structures. Zechmeister and Zechmeister (2000) looked at the glossaries of ten American introductory textbooks published between 1994 and 1997. They found that 49% of key terms only occurred in one text and that only 3% were identified in all ten. In a study of 24 American introductory texts Gorenflo and McConnell (1991) failed to find a single reference that was cited in all books.

There is also considerable variation in the sort of text features used in different books (Marek *et al.*, 1999); the only feature shared by all analysed texts being emboldened terms. Clearly then not all psychology textbooks are the same. This does not mean of course that there are necessarily substantial differences in *quality*, merely that all writers represent psychology as they see it and uses the sort of chapter features they believe to be pedagogically useful. Teachers may wish to consider which representation of psychology and which pedagogical aids they wish to go with. As Griggs and Marek (2001) conclude, research findings show that choosing textbooks is important and worth an investment of teacher time.

Qualitative critiques of psychology textbooks

While American textbook research has focused on their quantitative dimensions, qualitative studies in the UK have looked at the more subtle dimensions of psychology texts. Howitt and Owusu-Bempah (1994) focused on the use of racist language, exemplified by the use of the word 'tribe' in a leading American text. Words like 'tribe' are considered racist, because the term can refer both to humans and animals, but when referring to humans is always used to refer to black rather than white people. It thus constructs black people as closer to animals than to white people.

In similar vein Jarvis (2000) has deconstructed the language used to describe Freud in another leading American psychology text. Numerous examples were found of ways in which language can be used to bias a reader against a theory. For example the sentence 'Although Freud's current influence in psychological science is slight, his notoriety continues to colour people's perceptions of psychology, and his influence lingers in literary interpretation, psychiatry and pop-psychology' can be unpacked in a number of ways. Freud is being associated here with three out-groups, a rival discipline (psychiatry), an inferior discipline (pop-psychology) and an irrelevant discipline (literary interpretation). The terms 'notoriety' and 'lingers' are also significant in constructing Freud as an unwelcome and perhaps even criminal influence on psychology. The term 'psychological science' (not used elsewhere in the book) further serves to remind the reader that psychology is a science, and that Freud does not live up to the standards of science.

Pennington (2000) analysed a range of American introductory texts with regard to their claims to support critical thinking (see Chapter 4 for a discussion). All ten texts claimed in their prefaces to encourage critical thinking, seven giving an explicit definition. The developmental psychology sections were then looked at closely in order to assess how effectively devices were used to encourage critical thinking. The following weaknesses were noted:

- In some cases critical thinking questions were asked for which there was little or no relevant material in the text.
- Some questions were extremely vague and unclear.
- Some questions required value judgements or application rather than critical thinking. This is still higher level thinking but not *critical* thinking as defined in the books.
- Where sections of critical thinking are included in the text the work is done and an opportunity is not provided for students to think for themselves.

There are clear lessons from this study, both for teachers looking for effective textbooks and for those looking to devise resources with which to promote critical thinking. Students need to be given the tools with which to think about the material and appropriate material about which to think, but probably not the answers, at least in elaborated form. See page 69 for a discussion of strategies to encourage higher-level thinking.

Textbook study guides

Many modern textbooks come with an accompanying study or companion guide. This typically contains advice on how to study, breakdowns and summaries of syllabus material and self-assessments using a variety of formats. In the USA it is common practice to make psychology study guides required reading. As Dickson *et al.* (2005) point out, there are good reasons in terms of information processing theory to believe that study guides will be helpful; they require students to 'effortfully process and manipulate course material' (Dickson *et al.*: p. 34), and contain self-assessment questions the use of which is likely to maximise retrieval routes. Dickson *et al.* assessed the effectiveness of study guides with 236 undergraduate psychology students. In one condition students worked with a study guide and in the other a control group completed the same course without the guide. Those using the study guide did better on multiple-choice exams, and when surveyed, most students reported that they found study guides useful and would use them again. Cautiously, then, evidence does seem to support the usefulness of study guides.

Textual characteristics and pedagogical aids: what makes a good resource?

Clearly students need to be able to concentrate on, understand and remember text before it becomes a useful resource. There are a number of variables that can affect how easy a piece of text is to process. These range from the physical layout of the page, use of figures and pictures, etc., to the ways words are put together and the use of various pedagogical aids.

Page layout

This is an area plagued by poor quality research and misguided attempts to apply findings from one culture and age group to others. Studies of font readability for example have often not controlled for letter height or line spacing, both of which constitute confounding variables, and which the writer can alter. As in all things, do what works for you and your students rather than follow the dogma. The following suggestions are intended as some ideas worth trying, but I stress that they are based on limited empirical research.

- Try increasing line spacing slightly and compensate by taking the font size down a fraction. Several studies have found that line spacing is more important than font size in making text readable. An example is shown in Box 5.1.
- Try using unjustified text. This can make your resource look a little less slick but again research tends to find that unjustified text is easier to read. An example is shown in Box 5.2.

Box 5.1

The effect of varying font size and line spacing: which of these is easier to read?

Example 1. Times New Roman size 12, line space at 1 point

Bowlby noted that infants are born with a set of instinctive behaviours including smiling, sucking, gesturing and crying. He proposed that these have evolved in order to maximise the chances of being well looked after and hence surviving. Bowlby called these behaviours *social releasers*. Their function is to elicit instinctive parenting responses from adults. The interplay between social releasers and parenting responses is the process that builds the attachment between infant and carer.

Example 2. Times New Roman size 11.5, line space at 1.3 points

Bowlby noted that infants are born with a set of instinctive behaviours including smiling, sucking, gesturing and crying. He proposed that these have evolved in order to maximise the chances of being well looked after and hence surviving. Bowlby called these behaviours *social releasers*. Their function is to elicit instinctive parenting responses from adults. The interplay between social releasers and parenting responses is the process that builds the attachment between infant and carer.

Box 5.2

The effect of unjustified text: which of these is easier to read?

Example 1. Justified

Bowlby noted that infants are born with a set of instinctive behaviours including smiling, sucking, gesturing and crying. He proposed that these have evolved in order to maximise the chances of being well looked after and hence surviving. Bowlby called these behaviours *social releasers*. Their function is to elicit instinctive parenting responses from adults. The interplay between social releasers and parenting responses is the process that builds the attachment between infant and carer.

Example 2. Unjustified

Bowlby noted that infants are born with a set of instinctive behaviours including smiling, sucking, gesturing and crying. He proposed that these have evolved in order to maximise the chances of being well looked after and hence surviving. Bowlby called these behaviours *social releasers*. Their function is to elicit instinctive parenting responses from adults. The interplay between social releasers and parenting responses is the process that builds the attachment between infant and carer.

● Try inserting images into the text. Some studies have shown that students with a visual learning style (see Chapter 7 for a critical discussion of learning styles) find text easier to process if there are images present. An example is shown in Box 5.3.

Box 5.3

The effect of adding an image: which of these is easier to read?

Example 1. Without image

Bowlby noted that infants are born with a set of instinctive behaviours including smiling, sucking, gesturing and crying. He proposed that these have evolved in order to maximise the chances of being well looked after and hence surviving. Bowlby called these behaviours *social releasers*. Their function is to elicit instinctive parenting responses from adults. The interplay between social releasers and parenting responses is the process that builds the attachment between infant and carer.

Example 2. With image

Bowlby noted that infants are born with a set of instinctive behaviours including smiling, sucking, gesturing and crying. He proposed that these have evolved in order to maximise the chances of being well looked after and hence surviving. Bowlby called these behaviours *social releasers*. Their function is to elicit instinctive parenting responses from adults. The interplay between social releasers and parenting responses is the process that builds the attachment between infant and carer.

Text readability

How easy a piece of text is to read varies in line with several dimensions of the way it is worded. There is a range of formulae around which a readability index can be calculated. Typically these input variables such as sentence length, number of letters per word and number of syllables per word. For example the Fog Index is calculated using the following formula.

$$\text{Index} = 0.4(\text{words/sentences} + 100((\text{words} > 2 \text{ syllables})/\text{words}))$$

There are interactive websites that will calculate your readability indices for you. I recommend readability.info (http://www.readability.info/), because this gives scores using several different formulae and also reports on other variables that might impact on readability. These include the following:

- Use of the passive voice can make text harder to follow
- Conjunctions lengthen sentences and may make them harder to follow
- Too many pronouns can make meaning ambiguous, however too few tend to lead it to lack fluidity.

Box 5.4 shows how a piece of text of mine fairs when analysed for readability.

Box 5.4

Readability of a text extract

Bowlby noted that infants are born with a set of instinctive behaviours including smiling, sucking, gesturing and crying. He proposed that these have evolved in order to maximise the chances of being well looked after and hence surviving. Bowlby called these behaviours social releasers. Their function is to elicit instinctive parenting responses from adults. The interplay between social releasers and parenting responses is the process that builds the attachment between infant and carer.

Fog Index = 14.6.
The ideal is 7–8. A score of over 12 indicates that most people would find it hard to read.

0 long sentences.
2 short sentences.
Words >2 syllables = 14
Average syllables = 1.68

Source: Jarvis (2001)

Looking at the breakdown of the high Fog Index in Box 5.4 it seems that the problem is the number of long words. Box 5.5 shows the same text rewritten with the number of three-syllable words reduced. The Fog Index is now 10.8, within acceptable limits.

Box 5.5

Readability of a modified text extract

Bowlby noted that infants are born with a set of behaviours such as smiling, sucking, waving and crying. He proposed that these have evolved in order to improve the chances of being well looked after and hence living to adulthood. Bowlby called these behaviours social releasers. Their function is to trigger innate parenting responses from adults. The exchange of social releasers and adult responses is the process that builds the attachment between infant and carer.

Fog Index = 10.8.

Words >2 syllables = 9
Average syllables = 1.53

Making textual changes: coherence and linking

Although it can be very instructive to submit both your own handouts and the textbooks you use to readability analysis, there are other variables to take into account, and a readability index does not tell the whole story. Vidal-Abarca and Sanjose (1998) suggest two ways to enhance the readability of text that would not show up on a readability analysis. These are coherence textual changes and linking textual changes. *Coherence* textual changes involve improving the overall coherence of a passage, for example by adding headings and summaries, and by linking one idea to another. *Linking* textual changes involve explicitly linking new ideas to the reader's existing knowledge. Consider the passage in Box 5.6.

In Box 5.6, which introduces Vygotsky's theory of cognitive development, it can be seen that coherence is achieved by means of subheadings and a summary section. Linking is achieved by means of references to Piaget, with whom the reader is already familiar.

Box 5.6

A passage including coherence and linking changes

Vygotsky was writing at around the time of Piaget's early work. Like Piaget he believed that cognitive development occurs in stages and that each stage involves qualitatively different thinking abilities. However his theory differed in several key ways.

> Linking textual change

> Coherence textual change

The importance of culture and social interaction

Vygotsky placed far more emphasis than did Piaget on the role played by culture in the child's development. Vygotsky saw children as being born with basic mental functions such as the ability to perceive the outside world and to focus attention on particular objects. However, children lack higher mental functions such as thinking and problem solving. These higher mental functions are seen as cultural 'tools'. Tools are transmitted to children by older members of the culture in guided learning experiences (such as lessons in school), and include the ability to use language, art and mathematics. Experiences with other people gradually become internalised and form the child's internal representation of the world.

> Coherence textual change

The Zone of Proximal Development

In contrast to Piaget, who emphasised how much a child can learn by exploring its environment, Vygotsky put his emphasis on the fact that children can develop their understanding far more quickly while interacting with other people. Children, according to Vygotsky, could never develop formal operational thinking without the help of others. The difference between what a child can understand on its own and what it can potentially understand through interaction with others is called the Zone of Proximal Development (ZPD).

> Linking textual change

The role of language

Vygotsky placed far more emphasis on the importance of language in cognitive development than did Piaget. For Piaget, language simply appeared when the child had reached a sufficiently advanced stage of development. The child's grasp of language depended on its current level of cognitive development. For Vygotsky, however, language developed from social interactions with others and was a very important cultural tool. At first the sole function of language is communication, and language and thought develop separately. Later, the child internalises language and learns to use it as a tool of thinking.

> Linking textual change

Summary

Vygotsky emphasised the role of interaction with others in cognitive development, seeing higher mental processes as acquired from other people. He saw the limiting factor in development at any time as the presence or absence of a tutor. Language is an important mental tool internalised in contact with others and used for thinking.

> Coherence textual change

Emphasising key concepts: signalling and elaboration

Key concepts in a piece of text are said to be *signalled* when they are extracted and explained in detail in boxes. An example is shown in Box 5.7.

Nevid and Lampmann (2003) investigated the effectiveness of signalling. 80 college students read matched textbook passages with or without 'key terms' boxes. They were then tested on the material. Performance in the tests was better overall in the signalled condition. This was accounted for entirely by enhanced performance on the signalled areas, and there was no difference in test performance in the non-signalled content. This supports the usefulness of signalling.

Whenever key terms are defined, irrespective of whether they are signalled, we tend to elaborate on a definition, for example by paraphrasing it, giving an example or providing a mnemonic device to make it more memorable. Balch (2005) compared the usefulness of different types of elaboration in an experiment conducted on first year American psychology undergraduates. Participants received passages including definitions of 16 psychological terms, followed by either a paraphrase (e.g. 'a dissociative disorder is a psychological problem in which people may not remember certain events that happen to them or who they are'), an example (e.g. 'a person with a dissociative disorder might be found standing by the road somewhere without knowing how they got there, what their name is or where

Box 5.7

An example of signalling

Bowlby noted that infants are born with a set of instinctive behaviours including smiling, sucking, gesturing and crying. He proposed that these have evolved in order to maximise the chances of being well looked after and hence surviving. Bowlby called these behaviours *social releasers*. Their function is to elicit instinctive parenting responses from adults. The interplay between social releasers and parenting responses is the process that builds the attachment between infant and carer.

> **Key term: social releasers**
> Instinctive behaviours including smiling and gesturing, designed to elicit nurturing behaviour from adults

they live'), a mnemonic (e.g. 'the first two syllables of dissociative sound like disco. Discos are usually dark, and people with dissociative disorder are in the dark because of disruptions in the memory, consciousness or identity') or a repeated definition. They were then tested on the terms using multiple-choice questions. Examples and mnemonics were associated with improved performance in the test, however paraphrases and repeated definitions were not.

Comparing pedagogical aids

Gurung (2003) identified seven pedagogical aids commonly used in psychology textbooks. All of these can be used in teacher-generated resources:

- Chapter outlines
- Chapter summaries
- Emboldened terms
- Italicised terms
- Key terms
- Practice questions
- Quizzes.

Gurung went on to survey students about how often they made use of each of these aids and how useful they found them. Emboldened and italicised terms to make important terms stand out and quizzes and practice questions to help test learning were rated as the most helpful and commonly used features. Interestingly though, in a follow-up study (Gurung, 2004) it emerged that the use of such aids declined during a psychology course, suggesting that students may have initially overestimated their usefulness.

A checklist for assessing resources

Given how many variables appear to have an effect on how suitable psychological text is for students, whether in the form of a textbook or teacher-generated handouts, it is perhaps worth having a tool with which to examine such resources, in particular your own, which can be easily altered. This is not to suggest that all your resources should use all these devices all the time, just that if you are looking to improve them these ideas might provide ways forward. In that spirit I offer a checklist of text features and pedagogical aids. This is shown in Box 5.8.

Box 5.8

A checklist to assess text features and pedagogical aids in student resources

Page layout	Font size and line spacing are optimised	Text is unjustified	Images or diagrams are included	
Textual features	Fog Index is <12	Subheadings are used	Summaries are used	Links are made to prior learning
Pedagogical aids	Key terms are emboldened or italicised	Key terms are signalled	Key terms are elaborated	Questions are included

Resources that apply psychology to life

News stories

In Chapter 3 I suggested that learning can be improved by making it directly relevant to the lives of students, and that one way in which this can be achieved is by the use of articles from the press. Using contrived articles that only tenuously link to the psychology syllabus is probably counterproductive, but regular manual searches of the news are very labour-intensive. One way to locate news stories quickly and easily is by means of internet searches. This has the additional advantage that text can be quickly cut and pasted into a worksheet, making the exercise an efficient use of teacher time. Some examples of sites that can be used for locating news are shown in Table 5.1.

Once way of using news articles in student resources is to follow up the text of the article with a set of questions that encourage the reader to apply particular theories or research findings to explain what happens in the story. An example is shown in Box 5.9.

Table 5.1 Some sources of psychology-related news stories

Site	Description	Current URL
Psyseek	Links to *New York Times* psychology news	http://www.psyseek.co.uk
Google News	Searchable news search engine	http://news.google.co.uk
BBC	Searchable news site	http://www.bbc.co.uk
Psycport (APA news)	Psychology news site	http://www.psycport.com/
Yahoo Science News	Searchable science news site	http://uk.news.yahoo.com/505/
The *Observer*	Searchable news site	http://www.guardian.co.uk/

Box 5.9

An example of using a news story as stimulus material in a study of destructive obedience

'Do as you're told' by Nicci Gerrard. From *The Observer Review* 12 October 1997.

CP Snow wrote that 'more hideous crimes have been committed in the name of obedience than have ever been committed in the name of rebellion.'

In the early hours of 13 July 1942, the 500 men of the German Reserve Police Force Battalion 101 – middle-aged family men, too old for the army, barely trained, and stationed in Poland – were addressed by their leader, Commander Trapp. In a voice shaky with distress he told them of their next assignment: to seek out and kill the 1800 women and children in the nearby village of Jozefow. Then, astonishingly Trapp told them he knew what a repugnant task some might find it, and that anyone could stand out with no punishment and no reprisals. Out of 500, only 12 men stood out.

During that terrible day, a further 10-20% managed to evade their duty; many more became distressed but continued to carry out the orders. Quite a few exhibited no signs of distress. A few seemed to enjoy themselves.

We are necessarily bred into obedience the moment we are born. How else does a society operate? Politeness and embarrassment are important factors, as is the unwillingness to let someone down. The absorption in the technical aspects of the task makes us lose our sense of what we are doing. We easily fool ourselves that we are not to blame – divesting ourselves of authority and attributing it to a legitimate authority, so that we become a simple agent: 'I was just doing my job'.

Questions
1. What similarities can you see between the responses of the men of Battalion 101 and that of Milgram's participants?
2. What suggests that at least some of the men went into an agentic state?
3. It has been suggested that one of the weaknesses of Milgram's explanation of obedience is that it does not explain individual differences in behaviour. What individual differences can you see here and how do they affect your assessment of Milgram's explanation?
4. To what extent do you agree with Snow's idea that obedience causes more harm than rebellion?

Popular culture: from film to lyrics

There are a number of ways in which popular culture can be brought into the psychology classroom and used to enthuse students. The obvious approach is to show films containing psychologically relevant content. Green (2005) suggests that there are three good reasons to use film in teaching psychology:

- It allows teachers to make the same point in different ways, serving as an elaboration of the material covered in lessons.
- It makes psychological material directly relevant to real life and allows us to talk to students in their own language about aspects of their own culture.
- It can be used to develop critical thinking as students learn to debunk inaccurate portrayals of psychological topics in film.

Green offers the following advice to psychology teachers considering using film as a teaching aid:

- Watch the film in advance to check that it is relevant and does not contain offensive material.
- Watch the film with the class.
- Be aware of copyright laws.
- Don't feel obliged to watch a long film in full when only a section is of direct relevance.
- When a film takes a whole lesson follow it with a piece of related homework so that momentum is not lost by the next lesson.

Blair-Broeker (2002) adds an additional piece of advice – be very wary of the phrase 'based on a true story'! There is always a degree of artistic licence in the way films are put together. For example *A Beautiful Mind*, the touching story of brilliant mathematician John Nash's struggle with schizophrenia, contains entirely made-up elements that detract from the accurate portrayal of Nash's case and schizophrenia in general. A related issue concerns thinking carefully about what point you are using film to illustrate. Blair-Broeker gives the example of *Sybil*, a film based on a case of dissociative identity disorder (DID, formerly multiple personality disorder). *Sybil* is sometimes used to portray the nature of DID, however as Blair-Broeker points out, the content of *Sybil* best illustrates the constructive nature of memory and the power of therapist suggestions, thus the best use of *Sybil* in teaching is perhaps as an illustration of the debate over DID as a real disorder. Table 5.2 shows some examples of films useful for illustrating psychological material. This is adapted from Burden (1993), Blair-Broeker (2002) and Green (2005), and is intended to be illustrative rather than exhaustive.

Table 5.2 **Examples of films with themes relevant to post-16 psychology**

Film	Area of psychology	Psychological material illustrated
Monty Python and the Holy Grail	Defining abnormality	Diagnosis of witchcraft
Sybil	Defining abnormality	Existence of dissociative identity disorder
One Flew Over The Cuckoo's Nest	Defining abnormality	Diagnosis as social control
As Good As It Gets	Psychopathology	Obsessive compulsive disorder
Born On The 4th Of July	Psychopathology	Post-traumatic stress
Rainman	Psychopathology	High-functioning autistic spectrum disorder
A Beautiful Mind	Psychopathology	Schizophrenia
Fight Club	Psychopathology	Dissociative identity disorder
Nurse Betty	Psychopathology	Dissociative fugue
Hamlet	Psychopathology	Depression
The Horse Whisperer	Psychopathology	Depression
Henry: Portrait of a Serial Killer	Psychopathology	Antisocial personality disorder
Silence of the Lambs	Psychopathology	Antisocial personality disorder
I Am Sam	Psychopathology	Retardation
Analyse This	Psychoanalysis	Psychoanalytic psychotherapy
Star Wars	Psychoanalysis	Oedipus complex + Jungian archetypes
The Forbidden Planet	Psychoanalysis	Id/superego conflict
Memento	Memory	Anterograde amnesia
Total Recall	Memory	Retrograde amnesia
Boys Don't Cry	Relationships/homophobia	Treatment of a young lesbian
Gregory's Girl	Adolescence	Adolescent relationships
Rebel Without a Cause	Adolescence	Adolescent identity
American Beauty	Adult development	Midlife crisis
Alive and Kicking	Addiction	Heroin addiction
The Basketball Diaries	Addiction	Heroin addiction
Awakenings	Neurological disorder	Sleeping sickness
My Own Private Idaho	Neurological disorder	Narcolepsy

Television also provides opportunities to illustrate psychological material. Although often less profound and moving than feature-length films, TV episodes have the advantages that they are short and convenient. Table 5.3 shows examples of psychological material exemplified in *The Simpsons*.

Table 5.3 **Psychological themes in *The Simpsons***

Episode	Title	Psychological theme
Series 1 episode 2	Bart the Genius	Adjustment of children with high IQ
Series 1 episode 5	Bart the General	Bullying at school
Series 1 episode 6	Moaning Lisa	Depression and sublimation
Series 2 episode 9	Itchy and Scratchy and Marge	Media violence
Series 3 episode 1	Stark Raving Dad	Defining abnormality/psychiatric diagnosis
Series 3 episode 18	Separate Vocations	Psychometric testing
Series 4 episode 10	Lisa's first words	Language development
Series 4 episode 21	Marge in Chains	Kleptomania
Series 5 episode 4	Rosebud	Transitional objects (object relations)
Series 5 episode 9	The Last Temptation of Homer	Midlife crisis
Series 6 episode 3	Another Simpsons Clip Show	Relationships
Series 6 episode 8	Lisa on Ice	Sibling rivalry
Series 6 episode 10	Grandpa vs Sexual Inadequacy	Oedipus complex
Series 6 episode 11	Fear of Flying	Phobia of flying
Series 6 episode 24	Lemon of Troy	Robbers Cave experiment spoof
Series 7 episode 23	Much Apu About Nothing	Racism
Series 8 episode 15	Homer's Phobia	Homophobia
Series 9 episode 13	The Joy of Sect	Cults
Series 10 episode 2	The Wizard of Evergreen Terrace	Midlife crisis
Series 10 episode 16	Make Room for Lisa	Territoriality
Series 11 episode 2	Brother's Little Helper	ADHD
Series 13 episode 5	The Blunder Years	Recovered memories
Series 14 episode16	The Wandering Juvie	Adolescence

Film and TV are not the only media in which popular culture lends itself to psychology teaching. For those who teach prejudice and look at discursive or social constructionist approaches, deconstructing the lyrics of some contemporary music is a way to demonstrate the ubiquity of prejudice in language. A published study to use as a demonstration comes from Burns (1998), who deconstructed the lyrics to *Barbie Girl*. A brief account of the study is shown in Box 5.10.

Box 5.10

Deconstructing *Barbie Girl*

(Barbie) I'm a blonde bimbo girl
In a fantasy world
Dress me up
Make it tight
I'm your doll.

(Ken) You're my doll
Rock'n'roll
Feel the glamour and pain
Kiss me there
Touch me there
Hanky panky

(Barbie) You can touch
You can play
If you say
I'm always yours

Burns (1998) has revealed how some worrying beliefs about male-female relationships are expressed in these lyrics. Firstly, here is a discourse in which love, sex and ownership are closely linked together, suggesting that in fact ownership is a feature of sexual relationships. Barbie is constructed as a self-confessed blonde bimbo who describes herself as 'your doll', thus reducing herself to something less than a person (doll) and as the property of Ken (your). She offers herself as a sexual plaything (you can touch, you can play), on the condition that Ken gives a lasting commitment to her (if you say I'm always yours). Ken on the other hand is constructed as relatively unemotional. He makes no declarations of love, but instead demands sexual services (kiss me there, touch me there). Here is a representation of relationships in which women want love and men want sex and worse, in which men swap love for sex and women give sex in exchange for love.

Source: Jarvis *et al.* (2004).

Using this as a starting point students can deconstruct their own choice of lyrics. There are several internet sites (e.g. http://www.lyrics.com) where suitable lyrics can easily be obtained.

Assessment materials

A further category of resources that has not yet been mentioned is assessment materials. Clearly it is very important to familiarise students with the type of assessment materials they will come across in exams. However there are benefits to using a variety of assessment formats:

- Varying assessment formats can help keep student interest.
- Varying formats can also cater for a range of learning styles.

● Varying assessment formats may also maximise retrieval routes, making material more memorable (Dickson *et al.*, 2005).

Some of the common assessment formats are as follows:
● Essay
● Short answer question
● Multiple choice
● Cloze
● Crossword
● True/false.

Each of these formats is demonstrated below, and they are then compared. Each is concerned with the topic of obedience.

1. **Essay**: Critically discuss two studies of obedience.

2. **Short answer question**

(a) Describe the procedure of Milgram's classic study of obedience. (4)

....
....
....
....

(b) Outline Milgram's findings. (4)

....
....
....
....

(c) Critically consider the ethics of Milgram's study. (4)

....
....
....
....

3. **Multiple choice**

(a) Milgram's participants were
    a. children   b. men   c. women   d. men and women   e. dogs

(b) Mr Wallace is best described as a
    a. stooge   b. Iggy   c. stodge   d. stoolpigeon   e. stirrer

(c) The percentage of participants that gave 300 volts was
    a. 0%   b. 10%   c. 25%   d. 65%   e. 100%

(d) The percentage of participants that gave 450 volts was
    a. 0%   b. 10%   c. 25%   d. 65%   e. 100%

(e) Which was the most common reaction of participants
    a. distress   b. joy   c. sadness   d. amusement   e. indifference

4. Cloze

Milgram advertised for _____ volunteers to take part in a memory experiment
for a fee of $4. When the 40 participants arrived at the university, the
participants were told they would be either a teacher or a learner. They were
then introduced to 'Mr _____', a mild-mannered middle-aged man as a
fellow participant (in fact he was a stooge). By fiddling an apparently random
procedure, Milgram ensured that the participant was always the _____ and
'Mr Wallace' was always the _____. Mr Wallace was then strapped into a
chair and given a memory task involving remembering pairs of words. Every
time Wallace made a mistake Milgram ordered the participant to give him an
_____ _____. Of course there were no real shocks, but there was no way for
the participant to realise this. Following each mistake the level of the 'shock'
appeared to increase. The shock levels on the machine were labelled from
0–450 volts and also had signs saying 'danger – severe shock' and, at 450 volts
'XXX'. Milgram ordered participants to continue giving increased shocks
whilst the learner shouted and screamed in pain then appeared to collapse.
When participants protested Milgram told them 'the experiment requires that
you continue'. To Milgram's surprise, all the participants gave Mr Wallace at
least _____ (more than you would receive from the mains supply in Britain),
and ___% went the distance, giving the full 450 volts to an apparently dead Mr
Wallace! Most of the participants protested and some wept and begged in
their distress, obviously believing that they had killed Mr Wallace.

5. Crossword

¹W	I	T	²H	D	R	A	W	A	L	
			O							
	³J		H		⁴Y					
⁵H	O	L	O	C	A	U	S	T		
	N		H		L					
	E		O		E					⁶W
	S		F							A
			L				⁷S			L
		⁸M	I	L	I	G	R	A	M	L
			N				I			A
			G		⁹A	G	E	N	T	I	C
							H			E

Across

1. **WITHDRAWAL** – Milgram denied people this right when he told them they must continue
5. **HOLOCAUST** – Milgram's experiment was inspired by this
8. **MILIGRAM** – Lightweight obedience researcher
9. **AGENTIC** – State in which we obey – think Bond

Down

2. **HOHOHOFLING** – obedience researcher or a quick romp with Santa
3. **JONES** – The stooge patient in Hofling's study
4. **YALE** – The university where Milgram did his research
6. **WALLACE** – Not Mel Gibson, Milgram's stooge
7. **SMITH** – The doctor in Hofling's study

6. True/false

Identify each of the following statements as either true or false:

a.	Milgram's participants were working class men.	TRUE	FALSE
b.	Mr Wallace was one of the participants.	TRUE	FALSE
c.	There were 60 participants in the original study.	TRUE	FALSE
d.	100% of participants gave Mr Wallace 450V.	TRUE	FALSE
e.	Most participants were unhappy but obeyed Milgram.	TRUE	FALSE

The software needed to create slick versions of these formats is described in Chapter 6. Here we are more concerned with the educational implications of these formats. One thing to bear in mind is that different assessments rely on different aspects of memory; exam essays are tests of free recall, providing few cues. This means that students need to learn to write essay plans in order to cue themselves as they write in exam conditions. Short answer exercises are tests of cued recall and multiple choice and true/false exercises test recognition. Cued recall and recognition are easier than free recall, however these types of question leave no scope for the skilled writer to waffle. Crosswords and related tasks like wordsearches rely on a quite different type of information processing – what Gregorc (1979) has called *random* as opposed to *sequential* processing (this is discussed further in Chapter 7). This type of exercise often favours students who struggle with more logical sequential tasks, thus they can serve as encouragement for students with more unusual styles of information processing.

Summary and conclusions

Psychology teachers select from published resources and develop many of their own. It can therefore be very helpful to understand what makes a good resource. Textbooks have been the subject of a considerable body of research. No support exists for the sameness hypothesis – psychology texts vary considerably in both their content and use of pedagogical aids. There is a small body of research to suggest that well-constructed study guides can help students use textbooks. Understanding effective text is a surprisingly technical business, and it is perhaps worth teachers becoming familiar with aspects of text such as readability, coherence, linking, signalling and elaboration.

Resources are not always in verbal form and perform additional functions other than transmitting psychological information. Video material can be extremely useful in making psychology relevant to the lives of students. Films can be useful, however TV programmes are often shorter and illustrate the same points in condensed form – *The Simpsons* is particularly useful, illustrating psychological themes from the social consequences of hothousing to sibling rivalry, media violence, homophobia and the mid-life crisis. Another function of resources is assessment. There are a number of assessment formats, ranging from the traditional essay to crosswords. It is worth being aware of the different implications of these and using a variety of approaches.

Self-assessment questions

1. Discuss the idea that all psychology textbooks are much the same.

2. What criticisms have been made of psychology texts?

3. Discuss a range of text variables that may impact on how easy a text is to use.

4. How and why might film and TV be used in psychology lessons?

5. What formats can be used to assess psychology students? What implications do different formats have?

Further reading

•••••• Blair-Broeker, C. (2002) Bringing psychology to life. *Essays From e-xcellence in Teaching*, **2**, n.p.

•••••• Griggs, R.A. and Marek, P. (2001) Similarity of introductory psychology textbooks: reality or illusion. *Teaching of Psychology*, **28**, 254–256.

•••••• Rose, D. and Radford, J. (1993) *Teaching Psychology: Information and Resources*. BPS Books, Leicester.

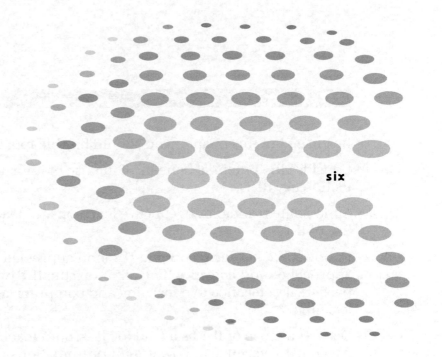

six

Using technology to teach psychology

Using technology to teach psychology

By the end of this chapter you should be able to:

- Consider the potential benefits of the use of information learning technology (ILT).

- Apply some principles of effective learning and teaching to the use of ILT.

- Define some key terms used in ILT, and appreciate the range of approaches and activities that fall under the ILT umbrella, with particular reference to e-learning and computer-assisted learning.

- Discuss the use of ILT as an aid to classroom teaching, with particular reference to PowerPoint presentations, demonstrations, simulations and experiments.

- Evaluate a range of statistical software and understand some of the issues attached to its use.

- Describe how resources including notes, links and test materials in a variety of formats can be used on an intranet.

- Understand how to create internet search tasks and use a range of on-line databases and specialist search engines.

One of the greatest social changes in the early 21st century has been the rapid development of computer-related technology. The importance of ICT (information and communication technology) is growing rapidly and many millions of pounds have been invested in bringing information technology to education. It is important to understand that there are two rather different purposes underlying this. The first is that students acquire a working familiarity with ICT in order to acculturate them to its omnipresence and better prepare them for the workplace. Pretty much any work involving computers is useful in this sense. However, there is a second and much more ambitious aim in actually enhancing the quality of learning by means of ICT. Former Education Secretary Charles Clarke put it thus: 'ICT can make a significant contribution to teaching and learning at all stages and across all areas of the curriculum. ICT should be embedded in all our education institutions and in all the teaching that takes place there' (Clarke, 2004, n.p.). The main aims of this chapter are to try to tease out some of the psychology of what might make ICT of direct benefit to learning, and to look in detail at how a range of ICT-related activities can be carried out. Clearly ICT hardware is expensive and software potentially so. Throughout this chapter my emphasis is on free software and free internet sites.

There is currently considerable pressure on teachers to step up their use of technology, and current progress has been too slow for the liking of politicians and ICT enthusiasts. Cognitive-developmentalist Seymour Papert (1996) has described teachers who favour the traditional classroom and who only cautiously use computers as 'cyberostriches'. Whilst it is certainly true that those of us who use little or no ICT in our teaching may be missing some tricks, there is also such a creature as the 'cyberlemming', who rushes into ICT use without consideration of the ways students learn. Many early initiatives failed because they assumed that students would adapt to technology rather than designing technology that played to the nature of human learning. We are now entering an era where this is better understood and where hardware and software are designed with an understanding of learning in mind.

Keeping the focus on principles of effective learning

However sophisticated our understanding of the technical side of technology we should always bear in mind that all technology is simply a set of tools, and that what we do with it should conform to principles of effective learning just like any other mode of teaching. Recall from Chapter 3 that, although we would be unwise to come out strongly for or against a particular model of teaching, we can abstract from education research a set of broad principles that underlie effective learning and teaching:

- Learning should be an active process rather than a passive process of taking in information. This is achieved when students use software themselves, for example searching, running simulations or analysing data with statistical software.
- Learning should be an interactive process. Interactions take place with teacher, peers and software. Teacher interaction can be in the form of whole-class discussions following the stimulus of a presentation or of scaffolding search, simulation and data analysis tasks.
- Learning should be made as relevant as possible to the learner. It is all too easy to get lost in search tasks that simply transfer from one metasite to another. ILT tasks must be focused either on bringing psychology to life or on developing course-related knowledge and skills.

- Learning should be memorable in order to prepare for exams. Material tends to be memorable when it has been deeply processed, visualised and when recall has been practised. Software can help with all these provided its use is well planned.

Understanding the language

If you are new to teaching or fairly new to using ICT in the classroom you will probably appreciate one systemic problem that has dogged the development of educational technology – the esoteric nature of the concepts and language used by ICT specialists. Historically this has meant that the overlap between those with a grasp of the technology and those with a good understanding of its applications to education has been relatively small. This in turn meant that in many cases the initial introduction of ICT to education was driven by the technically minded rather than the pedagogically wise, leading to expensive failures and a degree of teacher resistance. It is important for teachers to have at least a basic understanding of ICT and its educational applications if they are to take a role in shaping the role of ICT in future education. With that in mind the early part of this chapter is devoted to a brief overview of some of the major concepts.

ICT and ILT

There is an important distinction to be made between Information and Communication Technology (ICT) and Information and Learning Technology (ILT). As with many other modern technical terms, bear in mind that neither of these terms has been used entirely consistently in the literature (Taggart, 2004). Nonetheless in principle each has a distinct meaning. *ICT* is a generic term used to describe computing hardware and related communication technology such as telephone systems and networked computers. *ILT* is a fairly broad term that denotes 'the application of IT skills to learning situations using ICT' (National Learning Network, 2004, n.p.). In other words the focus in ILT is on ways in which to use ICT to enhance learning. As well as the obvious uses of PCs this includes the use of other devices such as interactive whiteboards.

Intranets

Delivery of ILT requires that information is organised and presented to the learner in a user-friendly manner. The most common way in which this is achieved is by means of an intranet. Leafe (2001) defines an intranet as 'a web or network-based system open to approved users' (2001: p. 182). It is now the norm for computers in schools and colleges to be networked. This has considerable advantage over individual PCs, allowing 'many users access to the same materials at the same time and enable knowledge, concepts and understandings to be communicated between many users. A teacher can display content as many times as there are machines available, enabling many pupils to access a single resource without huge photocopying costs. Content can be immediately updated, with updates available to all users' (2001: p. 185).

Multimedia and hypermedia

The term *medium* refers to the way in which information is brought to the user. Multimedia then simply means the use of multiple ways of storing and transferring information. When we speak of multimedia then we are really speaking of the accessing of educational software via CD-ROMs and the internet. *Hypermedia* describes the format of the learning material delivered by means of multimedia. Bruntlett (2001) defines hypermedia as 'text, animation, video, sound and images presented in high-quality digital resources.' The simplest form of hypermedia is hypertext. This is essentially text presented on multimedia, but with all the advantages this can bring over use of text in printed form. Material can be instantly cross-referenced from one source to another and several texts can be viewed simultaneously. Links can direct the reader to further sources, which may be differentiated according to level of understanding and the requirements of the particular task.

CAL, CBL and e-learning

There is a range of philosophies around as regards how ILT should be used. In particular there are debates about the extent ICT should fit into the traditional classroom and the extent to which it should shape the learning environments of the future. Although terms tend not to be used consistently in the ILT field we can broadly distinguish between computer-aided learning (CAL) and computer-based learning (CBL). Computer-aided learning takes place in a fairly traditional classroom. It might involve using a data projector and/or interactive whiteboard for whole-class exercises and perhaps a small suite of computers for more student-centred work. Computer-based learning, by contrast, takes place in a computer suite with most or all activities being done on computers. Currently (although of course this may change) most ILT developments are in the area of computer-aided learning and this is reflected in the emphasis in this chapter.

    E-learning has been defined as 'internet or intranet-based training that enables users to access training courses and learning materials on a desktop computer' (Training Press, 2001). This then has a narrower meaning, referring to the delivery of whole courses or substantial course elements using internet technology. This is variously supported by electronic or conventional tutorial elements. The main implication of e-learning is that it does not require a classroom. This makes it an excellent way to reach students who, by virtue of geography, time commitments or disability, cannot easily attend classroom sessions. Enthusiasts see e-learning as the way forward, replacing conventional teaching altogether. However there are serious potential problems with this scenario in terms of loss of peer interactions and the student-teacher relationship. Bolam (2004) makes an impressive case for the benefits of adopting an e-learning approach in a post-16 psychology department. He describes a model used in an independent girls' school in Jersey. This involved course materials being made available by e-learning, with conventional back-up of one lecture a week, one 'normal' lesson and a small-group tutorial. The benefits of this are described as follows.

- Students are accountable for their own learning.
- Small groups allow meaningful discussion.
- Free time is created so that marking can be completed in the working day.
- There is more time to give feedback to students.
- There is quicker and better development of the student-teacher relationship.
- Students complete more written work.
- There is more time to focus on skills as well as content.
- Gaps in understanding are quickly identified.
- Differentiation is easier to achieve because of the small group sessions

The current state of research doesn't really allow us to make generalisations about the rival merits of e-learning and computer-assisted learning. There are, however, some studies attempting direct comparisons. Mottarella *et al.* (2005) describes an experiment in which American psychology undergraduates took introductory modules in basic learning theory in one of three conditions: traditional classroom, web-enhanced and web-based. Those in the web-based condition did significantly worse than the other two groups. Other studies have found mixed results. Maki *et al.* (2000) compared exam grades and student satisfaction in an introductory psychology course taught by lectures and by interactive web-based software. The web-based condition was associated with better exam results but poorer student satisfaction. These findings illustrate the risks of embracing e-learning without elaborate and well thought out support, as was provided in the Bolam case study.

Presentation, simulation and observation technology

The remainder of this chapter is devoted to the use of ILT to support learning of psychology in the classroom and via intranet and internet. We are talking here about a huge range of software, from the humble PowerPoint for presentations to on-line simulations of experiments, graph-creating and inferential statistics packages, specialist academic search engines and meta-sites, and assessment-preparing packages. Almost all the downloadable software and interactive websites discussed here are free and fairly straightforward to use. Note that web addresses change and that when free software reaches a certain level of complexity it often ceases to be free. Some of the details given here will thus date fairly quickly. However, it should still give an idea of the range of material available to psychology teachers. Search engines will usually locate a new URL for an existing resource or an equivalent newer piece of free software without too much difficulty.

PowerPoint presentations

In the 1990s there was great enthusiasm for using PowerPoint as an alternative to the traditional board for delivering information. This was an excellent example of the cyberlemming phenomenon, and teachers soon realised that giving presentations in this way discouraged student activity and interactivity. There has now been a backlash against PowerPoint, criticisms being summed up in the bluntly titled article 'PowerPoint is evil' (Tufte, 2004).

- PowerPoint encourages simplistic thinking by summarising complex ideas on to a slide in the form of bullet points or graphs.
- PowerPoint is often used as a cue to remind a teacher of his or her next point rather than as an aid for the audience.
- PowerPoint encourages teachers to restructure content so that each idea fits on a slide.
- PowerPoint encourages classes to read material only in the order in which it is presented. This can be a disadvantage for students with particular learning styles.

As Daniel (2005) says, however, PowerPoint is just a tool, and examples of its poor use should not put us off attempting to use it properly. The current backlash against its use is therefore not really justified. PowerPoint is often best used for a short presentation prior to students beginning more active exercises. It is well suited to this task because it can display images and videoclips that can often make points more effectively than words on a board. If used for longer sessions there is no reason why a PowerPoint presentation should not include interactive exercises or links to imaginatively formatted self-assessment questions (page 122) and on-line simulations (page 114).

Online presentations and video clips

There is a plethora of PowerPoint lecture presentations available on-line. However it is well established that these are rarely if ever useful tools for the post-16 classroom. There are examples however of sites with extremely useful interactive presentations (especially good for biopsychology where visualisation of the nervous system is important) and video clips which illustrate studies better than pictures and verbal descriptions in textbooks. These will no doubt increase in number, although the URLs will probably change.* Some notable examples are shown in Box 6.1.

---

* I will endeavour to keep links up to date on www.mattjarvis.com

Box 6.1

Some examples of useful on-line presentations and video clips*

Description	Topic	Current URL
Video clip	Stanford Prison experiment	http://www.prisonexp.org/
Video clip	Milgram re-enactment	http://www.milgramreenactment.org/
Video clip	Language shaping	http://www.edu.uiuc.edu/courses/ edpsy313/mtpa/mtpaproj.htm
Video clips	Social learning	http://www.msstate.edu/VikiVideo/index.html
Interactive presentations	Neurophysiology	http://www.youramazingbrain.org http://www.bbc.co.uk/science/ humanbody/interactives/

* This is intended as an illustrative rather than exhaustive list.
With judicious searching you will be able to add to it.

The great advantage of interactive presentations and videoclips is that they take up very little classroom time and allow students to visualise things such as brain functionality and animal learning which are inherently interesting but can easily be made dry by too much verbal description. In terms of our criteria for effective learning this makes material both more relevant and more memorable. Of course video clips do not allow for much active student learning but they are usually short and can be followed by more active tasks.

On-line simulations and experiments

Also available on-line are a range of simulations and experiments which can be demonstrated in whole-class teaching via a data projector or performed by students in a computer suite. These also serve the function of bringing psychology to life but have the additional advantage that they involve students in active learning activities. Some examples of on-line simulations and experiments are shown in Box 6.2.

Some of these are metasites and link to several experiments or simulations. Be aware that when sites link to ongoing professional research projects (e.g. http://www.socialpsychology.org/expts.htm) there is considerable variation in the quality of feedback and debriefing provided to participants. Some topics researched on these sites are somewhat sensitive and may require vetting. Simulations and demonstrations of experiments are usually

Box 6.2

Some examples of on-line simulations and experiments

Description	Topic	Current URL
Parapsychology experiments	Zener cards, remote viewing, dice roll prediction, PK	http://www.parapsych.org http://www.mdani.demon.co.uk/para/psyc.htm
Memory experiments	Eyewitness memory Face recognition Word recognition	http://www.youramazingbrain.org.uk/testyourself/eyewitness.htm http://psychexps.olemiss.edu/Exps/demoold/aw5demo.htm http://psychexps.olemiss.edu/Exps/demoold/aw5demo.htm
Perception and attention experiments	Mental rotation Various illusions Dichotic listening	http://psychexps.olemiss.edu/Exps/demoold/aw5demo.htm http://psychexps.olemiss.edu/Exps/demoold/aw5demo.htm http://psychexps.olemiss.edu/Exps/demoold/aw5demo.htm
Clinical psych simulation	therapy with ELIZA	http://www.manifestation.com/neurotoys/eliza.php3
Learning simulations	Imprinting Classical conditioning Operant conditioning	http://samiam.colorado.edu/%7emcclella/expersim/expersim.html http://www.uwm.edu/~johnchay/cc.htm http://www.epsych.msstate.edu/adaptive/Fuzz/fuzzapplet.html http://www.uwm.edu/~johnchay/oc2.htm
Social psych experiments	Social facilitation Social perceptions Attitudes Implicit associations	http://samiam.colorado.edu/%7emcclella/expersim/expersim.html http://www.socialpsychology.org/expts.htm http://www.socialpsychology.org/expts.htm http://www.implicit.harvard.edu
Dreaming simulation	EEG, EMG and EOG	http://www.uwm.edu/~johnchay/sl.htm
Personal space simulation	The urinal game	http://flasharcade.com/game.php?urinal
Statistics simulations	Graphs simulations Correlation and regression simulations Numerous stats simulations	http://www.kuleuven.ac.be/ucs/java/ http://www.shodor.org/interactivate/activities/index.html http://noppa5.pc.helsinki.fi/koe/corr/index.html http://www.martindalecenter.com/ http://www.ruf.rice.edu/~lane/stat_sim/index.html

more straightforward. Be aware as well that some of these sites are much more straightforward to use than others. It is well worth exploring them yourself before letting students loose. As with all on-line resources, URLs go out of date. Most commonly this is because the institution hosting the material restructures its own website. A good tip to solve a non-functioning link is to go to the institution home page and search from there for what you want.

Recently the use of simulations has attracted the attention of researchers. Venneman and Knowles (2005) evaluated the benefits of *Sniffy Lite* (Alloway *et al.*, 2000, published by Thomson Learning). Sniffy is a virtual rat that can be conditioned to demonstrate various types of learning. The Lite version is simpler and Sniffy just undergoes classical and operant conditioning. In an experimental procedure Venneman and Knowles found that American psychology undergraduates using Sniffy outperformed a control group and rated Sniffy highly. Although versatile and reasonably good value (around £15 per machine), I found Sniffy to be lacking in user-friendliness and much preferred the simpler free on-line conditioning simulations shown in Box 6.2.

On-line webcams

Teaching observational research can now involve practical exercises without students having to leave their seats. There are numerous on-line webcams the output of which can be accessed over the internet (be a little cautious if you carry out a search for these as many hits will link to adult sites!). There are important ethical and legal issues to consider here. Under the Data Protection Act it is illegal to use surveillance techniques for anything other than security purposes and to do anything with that data other than keep it for a limited

Box 6.3

Some examples of zoos with live webcam feeds

Zoo	Observable animals	Current URL
Smithsonian Zoo	Ferrets, tigers, mole-rats, kingfishers, giraffes, pandas, octopus	http://nationalzoo.si.edu/Animals/WebCams/
Melbourne Zoo	Gorillas, butterflies	http://www.zoo.org.au/featured/webcams.cfm
San Diego Zoo	Polar bears, pandas, apes, elephants	http://sandiegozoo.org/videos/
Welsh Mountain Zoo	African birds	http://www.welshmountainzoo.org/camstream.htm

period and then destroy it, unless everyone that might be observed has given full permission. This means that although it is quite possible to access webcams in public places online it is *not* ethical. Even the observation of controlled situations like the Big Brother house, where observees will have given full permission and are aware they are being watched, raises some thorny issues. What is possible and ethically acceptable however is to use webcams in zoos to observe animal behaviour. Box 6.3 shows the URLs of some zoos that have live on-line webcam feeds. One tip for using zoo webcams is to bear in mind that they are frequently offline. Make sure that you have a few options lined up before starting a lesson.

Statistical software

Software that performs statistical analysis has been around in various forms since the 1960s. Early programmes tended to be unwieldy and required considerable knowledge of programming. Although many statistics aficionados still opt for this type of programme there are now a number of packages available with extremely user-friendly spreadsheet-type graphical user interfaces (GUIs). These perform a range of descriptive, graphical and inferential statistics. In the 1990s a low-cost and fairly user-friendly inferential stats package called stATPack was developed and sold by the Association for the Teaching of Psychology (Haworth, 1997). When stATPack was withdrawn after it emerged that some critical values were incorrect, the attention of psychology teachers shifted away from statistical software and has largely stayed away since.

However, much has changed since the withdrawal of stATPack. Most importantly, the internet has developed out of all recognition and with it has grown a movement for the free distribution of software, variously known as freeware, shareware and open source software (only freeware is *always* free, but often shareware and open source material will be made available free for educational purposes). In this climate it is quite straightforward to obtain statistical analysis software free of charge. Of course a lot depends on what we mean by 'free' (Grant, 2004). Although the software reviewed in this study is all free in monetary terms at the point of delivery, for a teacher exploring without help there can be considerable indirect costs in terms of the time required to track down, install and evaluate a range of packages.

One reason why little has been written about free statistical software in the psychology teaching literature is that universities have subscriptions to commercial packages – hence university staff can access very powerful and comprehensive software with comparative ease. The situation is very different in schools and colleges where budgets are far smaller. At the time of writing the UK 'industry standard' statistical package, SPSS, charges £995 per year for a site licence for the basic package. There are additional problems with using SPSS for teaching purposes. The tables of results generated for each analysis are unnecessarily complex (MacCrae, 2005, personal communication). We can easily be left having to sift through this for the information we want and feeling rather inadequate at how much of the information we don't understand! Another problem is that SPSS cannot be run on a network and must therefore be loaded separately on to each machine where it cannot be remotely accessed. Whilst all the free software reviewed here is ultimately less powerful than SPSS, much of it is probably better for post-16 level teaching simply because it is so much simpler and more comprehensible.

Jarvis (in press) has reviewed a range of free software designed to run inferential statistics tests. This includes both downloadable programmes and interactive websites. Twelve systems were assessed against the following criteria:

- Coverage of the inferential tests usually taught at post-16 level.
- Good range of additional tests for purposes of demonstration or teacher research.
- Resemblance to SPSS (i.e. good preparation for psychology at HE level).
- Ability to work with Excel files.
- Ability to run on a network.

Table 6.1 shows the coverage of the basic inferential tests commonly taught at post-16 level.

Table 6.1 **Coverage of inferential tests in free software**

Package	Chi^2	Sign test	Pearson's	Spearman's	t-test	Mann-Whitney	Wilcoxon
Downloads							
Merlin	✓	✓	✓	✓	✓	✓	✓
OpenStat	✓	✓	✓	✓	✓	✓	✓
Statlets	✓		✓	✓	✓		✓
PAST	✓		✓	✓	✓	✓	
SSP	✓		✓		✓		
Instat+	✓		✓		✓		
Statuccino			✓		✓		
Qmulate	✓		✓		✓		
SalStat	✓	✓	✓	✓	✓	✓	✓
AM			✓				
On-line							
VassarStat	✓		✓	✓	✓	✓	✓
StatCrunch	✓	✓	✓	✓	✓	✓	✓

Table 6.2 **Evaluation of free statistical software against other post-16 psychology criteria**

Package	Range of additional tests	Preparation for SPSS use in HE	Works with Excel files	Can be run on a network
Downloads				
Merlin	✓		Imports and exports as Excel files	✓
OpenStat	✓✓	✓✓	Imports and exports text files	✓
Statlets	✓	✓	Imports and exports text files	Not free version
PAST	✓✓	✓	Imports and exports text files	✓
SSP	✓			
Instat+	✓	✓	Imports and exports as Excel files	✓
Statuccino	✓			✓
Qmulate			Requires DOS commands	✓
SalStat	✓✓	✓	Imports and exports text files	✓
AM	✓	✓	Imports and exports as Excel files	✓
On-line				
VassarStat	✓		Cut and paste from Excel	N/A
StatCrunch	✓	✓	Imports and exports Excel files	N/A

Most packages were found to run Chi^2 and t-tests. Only Pearson's product moment was found in all programmes (although in the cases of SSP and Statuccino this had to be extracted from the regression function). Four packages were found to be complete in running all the inferential tests commonly taught at post-16 level. These were Merlin, OpenStat, SalStat and StatCrunch. Table 6.2 shows how well each package fared against additional criteria.

Three packages satisfied all the criteria against which I evaluated them. These were OpenStat, SalStat and StatCrunch. Merlin, VassarStat and PAST also emerged as extremely useful. All of these are thus recommended. Current URLs are shown in Box 6.4.*

OpenStat was developed by retired professor of psychology Bill Miller. It was designed with psychology in mind and carries out an enormous range of statistical tests. Its interface is virtually identical to that of SPSS, both in capabilities and layout. This makes it the best package for preparation for statistics at HE level. SalStat was developed by Cardiff

---

* These URLs are correct at the time of writing. They may change however. To keep up with new free stats packages try http://freestatistics.altervista.org/stat.php.

Box 6.4

Current URLs for recommended inferential stats software

- OpenStat http://www.statpages.org/miller/openstat/
- StatCrunch http://statcrunch.com
- SalStat http://prdownloads.sourceforge.net/salstat/SalStat.20031022.
  setup.exe?download
- VassarStat http://faculty.vassar.edu/lowry/VassarStats.html
- PAST http://folk.uio.no/ohammer/past/
- Merlin http://www.heckgrammar.kirklees.sch.uk/

University human-computer interaction expert Alan Salmoni. The interface is similar to OpenStat and SPSS in that it has a drop-down menu over a spreadsheet. Unlike OpenStat, SalStat can import and export to Excel without the hassle of converting to text files – a very useful timesaving feature. StatCrunch differs from OpenStat and SalStat in that it runs from an internet site rather than as a downloadable programme. Users need to register individually before they can access tests, but this is free and registered users can store files on the website if required. This can be particularly useful for students who wish to access files from home as well as an institution but who do not have remote intranet access. Merlin was developed by Neil Millar for Heckmondwike Grammar School, Kirklees. Although it was developed with biology A-level in mind it covers all the tests needed for post-16 psychology. Merlin differs from the other programmes reviewed here in that it is an Excel add-in. I find Excel a very clumsy statistical tool compared to the other packages reviewed here. This is not surprising as it is not primarily a statistical programme. However, for those who already use and like Excel it may be the package of choice.

More specialist research programmes

The packages reviewed above are primarily for inferential analysis, although they also include some descriptive table and graph functions. There also exists a range of more specialist software for particular types of research. This is less likely to be free and tends to be less user-friendly in design. Moreover to many teachers its use will be pretty marginal to post-16 teaching. However, in the spirit of sharing information that might be useful to someone I will mention three programmes here – these are shown in Table 6.3.

Table 6.3 **Examples of free specialist research software**

Title	Purpose	Current URL[*]
Lyons Morris	Meta-analysis of studies	http://www.lyonsmorris.com/lyons/metaAnalysis/index.cfm
TextSTAT	Content analysis of text	http://www.niederlandistik.fu-berlin.de/textstat/software-en.html
WebQ	Q-sort method	http://www.rz.unibw-muenchen.de/~p41bsmk/qmethod/webq/webqdoc.htm

It largely depends on what course, specification and options are being taken but a minority of post-16 psychology teachers might wish to make use of these, particularly content analysis. If several groups or classes are undertaking similar small-scale studies it may be worth meta-analysing them in order to demonstrate the technique.

Issues in the use of statistical software

Although there is no doubt that very good quality statistical software is available free of charge this is not to say that all teachers will be happy with using it. If the use of statistical software is not planned carefully there is probably a risk that it may lead students to use statistical methods without understanding them (potentially another cyberlemming scenario). On the other hand, in the current climate of packed specifications how much long-term benefit is there in students spending hours of precious classroom time learning to rank data? Personally I am horrified by the thought of students being put off psychology because they are intimidated by mathematical formulae, particularly when this is something they would never have to face as a professional psychologist. Even if we take quite a conservative line on the importance of teaching tests manually prior to using software (as is the norm in undergraduate psychology), being able to run inferential tests quickly and efficiently using software adds a whole new dimension to class practicals. It also gives students a taste of what undergraduate study will be like and it may help to lessen the culture shock of progression to Higher Education.

Resourcing a psychology intranet

Educational institutions typically have an intranet on which software, links and a range of support material can be placed. Obviously this is not mutually exclusive with the type of ILT materials discussed hitherto. Links to on-line simulations and presentations can be placed on an intranet as can statistical software. However many schools and colleges place additional material on their intranet, most often in the form of teaching notes and banks of questions.

[*] Correct at time of writing

Teaching notes

There is a healthy body of research into the benefits of placing teaching notes on the intranet, however this has been principally conducted in institutions of Higher Education. In one study for example Sutton (2000) surveyed students and lecturers at Southampton Institute about their practice of placing lecture notes and handouts on the intranet for students to access, and found very positive views. However, there are key differences in post-16 education that make this a more questionable practice. First, unlike HE lectures, lesson notes are not normally available in typed or presentation form. To type notes and put them on an intranet would be extremely labour-intensive. An additional problem is that making materials available independent of lessons is likely to encourage absenteeism – it becomes that bit more tempting to stay in bed knowing that one can 'catch up' by simply logging in to the intranet and downloading a set of notes. There are thus sound reasons to question the usefulness of this practice at post-16 level.

Assessment materials

A more popular and probably more productive use of intranet space in post-16 education involves self-assessment questions. Using (free) specialist software it is possible to construct these in a range of formats. This is important as students with different learning styles will probably respond differently to questions written in different forms (learning styles are discussed in more detail in Chapter 7). The most popular software for constructing test materials in the UK is Hot Potatoes, produced by Half-baked Software. There are, however, alternatives, notably SimpleSet from Question Tools. Both these packages produce files that can be directly uploaded to an intranet or website. Their features are compared in Table 6.4.

As these packages are free and have slightly different capabilities it is probably worth obtaining both. There are in addition more specialist packages available that just produce one test format. For example I find Eclipse Crossword much more user-friendly than the crossword function of Hot Potatoes. Of course, depending on your choice of specification and your judgements about the needs of your students, it may be possible to make use of on-line banks of questions. Box 6.5 shows some examples of these. As the development of all these sites is ongoing and rapid there is little point in describing their current capabilities in detail. Bear in mind when using and

Table 6.4 **Capabilities of *Hot Potatoes* and *SimpleSet***

Package	Survey	Cloze	True-false	Crossword	Multiple choice	Mix and match
Hot Potatoes		✓	✓	✓	✓	✓
SimpleSet	✓		✓		✓	

Box 6.5

Examples of sites with on-line question banks

Title	Owners/developers	Current URL
Psyweb	Nelson Thornes	http://www.nelsonthornes.com/courses/psyweb/
Psyonline	A consortium of schools	http://psyonline.edgehill.ac.uk/
Psychology Together	Psychology Together	http://www.Psychologytogether.com
Gerard Keegan	Gerry Keegan	http://www.gerardkeegan.co.uk
Psychlotron	Psychlotron	http://www.psychology.pwp.blueyonder.co.uk/

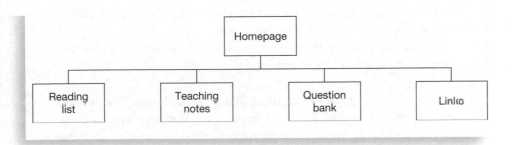

Figure 6.1 **An example of a department intranet site map**

recommending these that their content is not usually subject to the same rigorous peer review processes that characterise the development of books and journal articles, therefore they may contain factual errors.

The internet as a search tool

As we have already seen, the internet provides a wealth of resources for the psychology teacher, ranging from freeware, simulations and experiments to statistical analysis, question banks and webcams. Oddly, you might think, one of the harder things to do using the net is to find information! As a source of information about psychology the net has great potential but can be extremely frustrating. On the one hand, web browsers such as Internet Explorer have provided an unprecedented opportunity for students to explore the world, asking their own questions and seek their own sources of information (Churach and Fisher, 2001). On the other hand, most exploration using the net tends to be superficial (Selinger, 2001), students simply locating and re-presenting pre-existing materials rather than making the decisions and following lines of enquiry that would make searching a constructive task.

To use the internet effectively to find information, psychology teachers need to consider two things: first, what information they and their students are searching for and for what purpose; second, how are they going to go about it? Search tasks must be carried out with a particular purpose in mind. The obvious internet task that most of us start out by setting is very general in nature and uses a conventional search engine. However this approach typically results in the following problems:

- There are a huge number of hits and it is unclear which ones to follow up.
- Typically, each site has a small volume of information that rarely goes beyond what is in student textbooks.
- Many sites are of very dubious quality, containing incorrect information or with a 'pop-psychology' focus.
- Many sites are actually metasites, most links from which simply connect to each other, leaving the searcher going around in circles.
- Just as the search looks like it is getting somewhere it becomes apparent that the searcher either needs access codes or a credit card to get to the worthwhile information.

On-line searches are commonly conducted during coursework, when the topic of study often diverges slightly from the specification, leaving students struggling to find background information for introductions. Another reason is to back up existing notes with additional detail. For these purposes one of the most useful types of information is abstracts and the full text of studies. Psychology students in Higher Education and professional psychologists use on-line databases, in particular PsycINFO (abstracts only) and PsychARTICLES (full text of original papers), produced by the American Psychological Association. Unfortunately these require access codes, the cost of which is beyond the budget of most schools and colleges. However, students can locate a good range of abstracts and a smaller number of full text articles using a selection of free on-line databases and specialist search engines. Examples are shown in Box 6.6.

The detail and quality of abstracts varies considerably from one journal to another. In some cases they will provide enough detail for students to work from; in others they will not. However the British Library (http://direct.bl.uk/bld.Home.do) will now provide the full text of any article within a day or two for a small fee, so these search facilities are still useful for locating articles. One of the great advantages of using databases and specialist search engines is that they require students to actively make decisions about which key words to search for, which hits to follow up, what to print out, etc. Students working together can jointly take decisions. Thus this type of searching is an authentic constructivist activity (see page 42) for a discussion). For teachers and students looking to quickly locate the original full text of classic papers and books free of charge, an excellent site

Box 6.6

Examples of free on-line databases and specialist search engines

Title	Description	Current URL
MEDLINE	Database of abstracts	http://www.pubmed.gov
Ingenta	Database of abstracts	http://www.ingentaconnect.com/
Google Scholar	Specialist search engine	http://scholar.google.com/
PsychCrawler	Specialist search engine	http://www.psychcrawler.com/
Scirus	Specialist search engine	http://www.scirus.com/srsapp/

is York University's *Classics in the History of Psychology*, located at http://psychclassics.yorku.ca/.

Summary and conclusions

Following some notable early failures and false starts, ILT is now firmly established as an important part of education, and we are at the point where a good range of software is available which takes proper account of the way students learn. The time is thus probably right to firmly embrace ILT. That said, it is very important to bear in mind that ILT is simply a tool, not an end in itself, and careful thought needs to be given to using technology in ways that facilitate active, interactive, relevant and memorable learning. Neither a cyberostrich nor a cyberlemming be! One model for the use of ILT is e-learning, in which substantial percentages of courses are delivered via an intranet or the internet. Although there are now impressive case studies around showing that e-learning supported by good conventional tutoring can be effective, most institutions have focused on computer-assisted learning, in which ILT is used to support the conventional classroom. There is now an impressive range of programmes available to support CAL, including presentations, video clips, simulations, experiments and webcams. Good quality user-friendly statistical software is now also available. Critically, the vast majority of the best ILT resources are available free of charge via the internet, either as downloadable software or on interactive websites.

Two of the major challenges facing psychology teachers are effective use of intranets and the internet. A good strategy for keeping an intranet manageable is by the judicious use of links, for example to sites providing banks of questions. The internet as a source of information about psychology can be a great source of frustration, and some of the best specialist searching resources are expensive. However, judicious use of meaningful search tasks using free on-line databases and specialist search engines can help get around this.

Self-assessment questions

1. What are the potential advantages and pitfalls of using ILT?

2. Discuss the e-learning model of ILT.

3. Using examples, outline the use of on-line interactive presentations, videoclips, simulations, webcams and experiments.

4. Discuss the availability and usefulness of statistical software.

5. What sort of materials might go on to the psychology area of an intranet?

6. Explain how the internet can be used effectively as a tool for obtaining psychological information.

Further reading

•••••• Bolam, P. (2004) A case study on the development and use of an e-learning initiative. *Psychology Teaching*, Summer 2004, 39–45.

•••••• Jarvis, M. (in press) A systematic review of free statistics software: what works for post-16 psychology? Submitted to *Psychology Teaching*.

•••••• Leask, M. (ed) (2001) *Issues in Teaching Using ICT*. Routledge, London.

•••••• http://www.mattjarvis.com

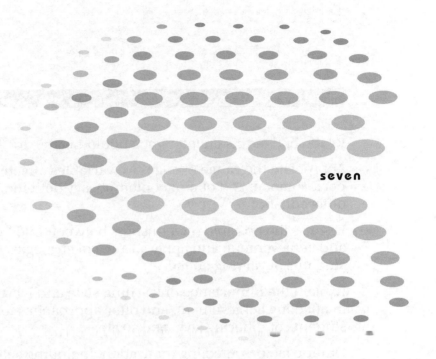

seven

Differentiated psychology teaching

Differentiated psychology teaching

learning objectives

By the end of this chapter you should be able to:

- Appreciate the range of cognitive variables affecting student performance, and offer a contemporary definition of differentiation.

- Discuss the possible relationships between intelligence, ability and achievement, and apply a range of strategies to help students of varying ability.

- Explain the importance of learning style and learning strategies in affecting achievement, and offer approaches to working with students of differing style and strategy.

- Outline factors affecting motivation, including self-efficacy and attributions, and suggest strategies to enhance motivation.

- Identify gender issues in the psychology curriculum, resources and classroom, and discuss how gender can impact on achievement.

Like virtually any group of people, psychology students are extremely diverse and so have differing needs. Pause a moment and think about just how many variables may impact on a student's experience of studying psychology. Aside from demographic factors such as age, gender, socio-economic status, ethnicity, culture and subculture, religion, sexual orientation and disability, we also need to think about the importance of individual cognitive differences, for example in intelligence, learning style, learning strategy and motivation. Thinking about consciously catering for all these variables all the time is likely to bring on cognitive overload! However, planning with diversity in mind can improve the experience of all students. As Ocampo *et al.* (2003) have pointed out, teachers and students within psychology – a discipline devoted to improving quality of life – should embrace efforts to improve the experience of studying for all. For teachers there is little doubt that this brings both additional challenges and rewards.

There is do doubt that work needs to be done to improve the way in which the diverse needs of students are met. The quality of a student's experiences may be affected by a number of planning decisions made about the running of a psychology course, including the curriculum, teaching methods, participation in research, assessment, skills training, teacher-beliefs and provision of student support (Zinkiewicz and Trapp, 2004). The processes of catering for diverse student needs fall under the umbrella of *differentiation*. This chapter addresses differentiation by ability, learning style, learning strategy, motivation and gender.

Defining differentiation

Although the concept of differentiation has been around for a while, its meaning has changed over time. A traditional definition of differentiation involves providing alternative resources and activities for students of differing ability. Whilst doing this may well form a part of a differentiation strategy, more modern and sophisticated views of differentiation depart from this tradition in two ways. First differentiation is now widely seen as being according to student *need* rather than ability. Ability may be one of the variables taken into account in differentiating, but other factors such as learning style, learning strategy, motivation and gender can be equally important. Second, differentiation need not mean providing *separate* tasks and resources for different groups, merely that the range of tasks and resources we use are suitable for a range of students. So how do we take account of these variables? For quality assurance purposes there are no prescribed differentiation strategies, although Ofsted require evidence that teachers are aware of individual differences in student needs and that assessments are used to inform individuals of their progress. BECTA (2003) suggests four strands to differentiation:

- Differentiation by resource: using resources that are accessible to a range of students.
- Differentiation by task: setting tasks that are suitable for a range of students.
- Differentiation by support: providing support mechanisms suitable for a range of students.
- Differentiation by response: providing feedback that identifies student characteristics and suggests ways forward.

These four strands of differentiation run through this chapter.

Ability and intelligence

It is a truism that students vary in their ability to successfully negotiate the sort of assessments made in post-16 psychology. Common sense suggests that one factor impacting on this ability to perform in psychology is intelligence – in fact as teachers we are often guilty of confusing ability and intelligence. Psychology teachers however should know better than to trust common sense – actually there is a surprisingly small body of evidence to suggest that intelligence (at least, as measured by IQ tests) is related to achievement in psychology, and even this needs unpicking further before the true relationships are revealed. In one recent study Diseth (2002) assessed 89 Norwegian psychology students for IQ using the Wechsler scale (WAIS). Only the vocabulary subscale of verbal intelligence predicted achievement in psychology exams. This relationship is perhaps not surprising – psychology is a language all of its own so we would expect success to be linked to vocabulary. The Diseth study is particularly important in demonstrating that intelligence and academic ability are not synonymous or even necessarily particularly closely related.

Anecdotal evidence suggests that post-16 teachers are now teaching students with a wider variety of ability and/or intelligence than was once the case. Certainly, given that intelligence (at least as measured by IQ tests) is normally distributed, it follows that with increases in the numbers of students we are now teaching some students with lower IQs than used to be the case (Rust and Golombok, 1999). This means that it is becoming increasingly important to use teaching strategies that are appropriate for students with a range of abilities. This need not involve rethinking all the ways you teach, just being aware of their significance. Consider the ideas discussed in this book. Co-operative learning and peer-tutoring allow students of currently low ability to pick up skills from peers. Problem-based learning tasks and references to popular culture allow students unused to or uncomfortable with thinking in abstract terms to make concrete psychological concepts. When we teach psychological thinking we are not merely drilling students for AO2 questions, but actually developing the skills needed to take their psychological understanding to another level. By considering textual variables we can construct student resources that are no less conceptually advanced but far more accessible to students with a range of reading ability. When we use ILT we are shifting away from the traditional classroom with its historical connotations of class distinction towards a more modern and egalitarian system. Box 7.1 summarises strategies to help cater for a range of current ability.

Implicit theories of intelligence

One theme emerging from the last section is that talking in terms of student ability and linking this to intelligence causes problems because in the Western world we have a tendency to see these variables as unchangeable. This is in contrast to attitudes in other cultures where intelligence is closely linked to effort and motivation. It may be then that when it comes to understanding

Box 7.1

Strategies to differentiate by ability

- Focus on developing skills. Much of the disparity between 'high-ability' and 'low-ability' students is not in their intelligence but their mastery of cognitive and metacognitive skills such as question analysis, planning and critical thinking. These can all be taught.
- The wider the range of current ability in a teaching group the more time should be spent in student-centred activities that allow students to work at their own pace.
- Consider using group work in which currently high- and low-achieving students are put together and consider implementing a programme of peer tutoring.
- Experiment with manipulating text variables and pedagogical features and see whether resources can be made more user-friendly.
- Make reference to popular culture. This helps link what can be very abstract principles to the everyday experience of students.
- Use more ILT. There is emerging evidence that ILT serves as a leveller between students of differing socio-economic status.
- Visibly adopt the attitude that ability is not fixed but changeable.

student achievement, intelligence *per se* is less important than what students believe about intelligence. We owe much of our understanding of this *implicit theory of intelligence* phenomenon to American psychologist Carol Dweck and her colleagues, who distinguish between entity and incremental theories. *Entity* theorists see intelligence as fixed whereas *incremental* theorists see it as changeable. Bandura and Dweck (1981) noted that their students were preoccupied with their intelligence and speculated that this appeared to be related to their belief that intelligence was a fixed quantity. The idea that we have a limited quantity of intelligence and that it may or may not be enough to achieve our goals naturally makes students anxious and can be demotivating. If we share this idea then we are unlikely to encourage students currently not achieving highly to do so. Dweck *et al.* (1995) developed a tool for measuring students' implicit beliefs about intelligence. The Implicit Theories of Intelligence Scale is shown in Box 7.2.

Studies have consistently shown that incremental beliefs are associated with high achievement (see for example Faria, 1998), and even that they can be more predictive of academic achievement than IQ. Studies have also shown that students from lower socio-economic groups are more likely to adopt an

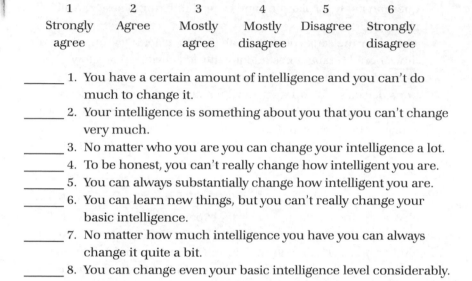

Box 7.2

The Implicit Theories of Intelligence Scale (adult version)

Read each sentence below and write alongside the number that shows how much you agree with it. There are no right or wrong answers.

1	2	3	4	5	6
Strongly agree	Agree	Mostly agree	Mostly disagree	Disagree	Strongly disagree

_____ 1. You have a certain amount of intelligence and you can't do much to change it.

_____ 2. Your intelligence is something about you that you can't change very much.

_____ 3. No matter who you are you can change your intelligence a lot.

_____ 4. To be honest, you can't really change how intelligent you are.

_____ 5. You can always substantially change how intelligent you are.

_____ 6. You can learn new things, but you can't really change your basic intelligence.

_____ 7. No matter how much intelligence you have you can always change it quite a bit.

_____ 8. You can change even your basic intelligence level considerably.

To obtain a score, add up the numbers from questions 1, 2, 4 and 6, and the reverse scores (6 = Strongly agree; 1= Strongly disagree) from 3, 5, 7 and 8. You will have a score between 8 and 48. The higher your score the more of an incremental theory you have.

Source: Dweck (2000)

entity theory (Faria and Fontaine, 1997). This points towards a practical application in improving the motivation of working class students. It is perhaps even more important to see academic ability as changeable. If IQ is to some extent modifiable, academic ability is surely more so – developing higher level thinking skills (Chapter 4) and revision strategies (Chapter 3) can transform students' ability to achieve in post-16 psychology beyond recognition. It is essential, though, that psychology teachers adopt an incremental position – if we don't believe we can transform academic ability then there is little incentive to work on student skills.

Dweck's work has further implications for challenging student stereotypes. Levy *et al*. (1998) gave college students an article (fictitious) that made a strong case for either entity theory or incremental theory. The students then undertook an apparently unrelated task of assessing the accuracy of stereotypes of ethnic and occupational groups. Those who had read the entity theory article concurred with the stereotypes to a much greater extent than those who had studied the incremental article. This and related studies suggest that successful challenging of entity beliefs in students can have a direct impact on their social development.

Learning styles and strategies

The last two decades have seen a growing appreciation of the fact that students vary not just quantitatively as a function of their ability (however we conceive of that), but also *qualitatively* according to the ways in which they process information and orient towards different subject matter, teaching style, study habits and mode of information presentation. For example, following on from the Piagetian tradition, teachers have tended to see orientation towards concrete rather than abstract ideas as cognitive immaturity or low intelligence. A more modern and less pejorative interpretation is that a student with a strong preference for concrete ideas is demonstrating a particular information-processing style. Table 7.1 shows some scenarios in which learning style might affect the study of psychology.

Looking at the scenarios shown in Table 7.1 two of the problems facing those working with learning styles leap out. First, to explain different

Table 7.1 **Using learning styles to explain common problems**

Scenario	Possible learning styles interpretation	Classification system
Jo has difficulty making sense of extended prose. When she sees psychology in diagrammatic form however it presents no problems.	Jo has a visual rather than a verbal learning style.	Riding (1991) Felder and Silverman (1986)
Will has no problem understanding psychological studies but has difficulty with more abstract theoretical ideas.	Will has a concrete rather than abstract learning style.	Gregorc (1979)
Amy gets on well with exam questions that are based on real-life scenarios or which have a lead-in quote but finds questions on their own out of a context confusing.	Amy is highly field-dependent, and is disadvantaged in the exam system as against more field-independent students.	Witkin (1964)
Chris studies straight sciences. In psychology he enjoys research methods, biopsychology and learning theory. He is however stumped by Freudian theory and social constructionism.	Chris has an analytic or sequential learning style, as opposed to a global or wholist style, and copes with logical progressions of ideas better than 'big picture' issues.	Riding (1991) Felder and Silverman (1986)

scenarios we need a number of classifications of learning styles. In the broadest sense of the term, all qualitative variations in learning can be thought of as learning styles, but this lack of precise definition is also a problem because it means that there is little agreement about what learning styles actually are (Reynolds, 1997). In their recent review Coffield *et al.* (2004) identified 71 distinct learning styles classifications of which 13 could be classified as 'major models' based on their theoretical importance, widespread use and influence on the development of later models. A second problem is that although we can interpret the problems these students are having by means of a particular learning style, it is hard to know whether this is the correct interpretation. The theoretical basis of learning styles is thus very weak, although they undoubtedly exist.

There are additional problems with the learning styles construct. We cannot currently measure learning styles in a reliable or valid way; the psychometric properties of learning style instruments vary widely and they usually fail to meet the standards of reliability and validity attained by standard IQ and personality trait inventories. In addition – forget the grand claims made by commercial dealers of learning styles packages – there is no consensus among researchers about the best way to respond to student learning styles. Typically, teachers receive feedback about each student and recommendations for how best to cater for their needs. This makes the assumption that student learning can be enhanced when teachers modify their style to fit more closely with the learning style of their students. However there is no clear evidence that this is helpful for the student (Pheiffer *et al.*, 2003).

Applications of learning styles research

Much of the research and practice currently carried out based on learning styles is probably little more than pop psychology. So has anything useful come from learning styles research? Actually I would suggest that there are three potential benefits to thinking in terms of learning style. First, the idea of learning styles encourages teachers to think about students in terms of meeting their differing needs as opposed to labelling their ability. Second, it encourages teachers to employ a variety of teaching and assessment methods in order to cater for students with different learning styles – this variety is almost certainly beneficial. For example we can easily make use of pictures, diagrams and graphs to encourage visual processing (the visual-verbal distinction is probably a robust one – see Riding and Rayner, 1998).

Finally, there are instances in classroom teaching when learning styles research can inform our feedback to students to their benefit. For example there is research suggesting that psychology students with a visual (as opposed to verbal) learning style particularly benefit from the use of ILT in

Box 7.3

Strategies to differentiate by learning style

- Avoid wholesale screening for learning style. There may be labelling effects and there is little evidence to suggest that teachers can respond effectively. A specialist can assess concerned individuals.
- Try using images in resources. This may benefit highly visual learners.
- Use a variety of teaching methods. Although we don't really know that particular teaching methods benefit students with particular learning styles variety is probably helpful to all.
- Try to think of students in terms of specific strengths and weaknesses (call these learning styles if it is helpful), rather than assign a label based on general ability.
- Consider referring students whose learning style appears to cause them a problem in psychology to a study skills unit.
- Consider offering feedback to students informed by learning styles research (possibly though not necessarily based on their own learning style).

lessons (Smith and Woody, 2000). We can respond to students who are aware that they have a strongly visual learning style (or indeed one who appears to be thrown by extended text) by suggesting that they make more use of ILT in their private study. Research also shows that students with a sequential as opposed to global learning style often orient to science subjects and are thus more likely to be comfortable with the hard science aspects of psychology. It can be helpful to spot this and work to prevent disenchantment with psychology, suggesting to the student something along the lines of 'you don't like Freud much'; 'you do sciences, don't you?'; 'hang in there, most of the course is more scientific than this'. No explicit reference to learning styles is needed for this type of intervention, merely an awareness informed by an understanding of learning styles.

Learning strategies

Learning strategies are patterns of learning behaviour. They are not subject to the same problems as learning styles, being conceptually clear, reliably measured and with clear implications for improving learning. Noel Entwistle and colleagues (e.g. McCune and Entwistle, 2000) have looked at three dimensions of learning strategy: deep learning, surface learning and strategic learning.

The distinction between deep and shallow learning has its roots in the cognitive psychology of the 1970s. In their *levels of processing* model of memory, Craik and Lockhart (1972) distinguished between information that is extensively processed for meaning (i.e. deeply processed) and is well remembered, and that which is processed less extensively for more surface attributes like sound or appearance (shallow processing). Entwistle *et al.* (1989) applied this idea to education, distinguishing between processing academic information for its surface attributes, and study using deep processing strategies. Shallow or *surface* learning involves relying on single sources of information and learning key points by rote. Learners adopting a surface strategy limit what they study and learn to the strict requirements of a syllabus. Deep learning by contrast is characterised by the motivation to understand the material being studied at as deep a level as possible.

A further dimension of learning strategy concerns how *strategic* learners are. Strategic learners are effective in organising their time and sources of information. They monitor the effectiveness of their strategies and are adaptable when their achievements do not live up to expectations. Nisbett and Shucksmith (1986) have described strategic learners as having a 'game plan' when approaching an academic task comparable to that of a football team approaching an important match. Box 7.4 shows the characteristics of strategic learning.

Applications of learning strategies research

If students who score highly in strategic and deep learning do better in psychology then it follows that enhancing deep and strategic learning should improve student performance. As a starting point it is certainly helpful to identify poor study habits. However, an over-reliance on surface strategies is associated with motivational factors, and we cannot assume that these can be consciously modified simply in response to seeing the results of a learning

Box 7.4

Activities of strategic learners

- Creating a plan of action
- Selecting appropriate strategies
- Implementing the strategies in order to carry out the plan
- Monitoring progress and modifying the strategies or even the plan, as appropriate
- Evaluating the outcome to inform future learning experiences.

strategies test. To develop deep learning strategies in learners we would have to impart to them a love of knowledge and thus the intrinsic motivation to study. There are of course opportunities to achieve this, for example at the start of post-16 education when students opt for subjects that particularly interest them. Although not currently researched, the transition from compulsory to post-compulsory education might be an excellent stage at which to build deep learning strategies. Currently research into deep learning has been focused on undergraduates, and has found that insight into learning strategy is associated with modest change. McCune and Entwistle (2000) followed up 19 psychology undergraduates over the course of their first year at university, to see whether they managed to modify their learning strategies. It emerged that, although some students made some significant changes, in general learning strategy proved quite difficult to modify.

Strategic learning may be more open to modification than deep learning. Strategic learning can be developed by the use of metacognitive strategies, i.e. approaches to teaching which make clear to students how and why they are learning. This is explicit in vocational courses such as GNVQ and AVCE where learners are regularly required to draw up action plans, name the strategies to be used, gather information and review the task. This 'plan, do and review' approach is closely related to the key activities of strategic learners shown in Box 7.4. Learners can also be taught time-management strategies, for example using timetables with evenings and weekends blocked so that quality study time can be built into the week. Fisher (1995) has suggested that even quite young students can be taught how to plan by means of providing appropriate examples of plans. He suggests a three-stage strategy for teaching planning:

1. Direct instruction stage: teacher explains planning and shows students examples of plans.
2. Facilitation stage: students put plans into their own words.
3. Self-generation stage: students construct their own plans.

Motivation

The term 'motivation' can be defined as 'the forces that account for the selection, persistence, intensity and continuation of behaviour' (Snowman and Biehler, 2000: p.371). In other words it is the sum of the influences that affect why we choose to behave in particular ways. A common lament among teachers is that their students are not motivated, but this is technically incorrect: students are always motivated, just not always to do what we want when we want it and in the way we see fit! Clearly though, it is generally in students' interests to work as their teachers wish them to. A number of factors influence this. We can look here in particular at two factors, students' self-efficacy and their attributions of success and failure.

Self-efficacy

Self-efficacy refers to our perceptions of our ability to carry out a task (Bandura, 1986). This is not the same as self-esteem, although they may impact on one another. Self-esteem is an emotional experience, describing the extent to which we like ourselves. It is also a global experience – our self-esteem is fairly constant across a range of situations. By contrast, self-efficacy exists within the cognitive domain, describing our *beliefs* rather than feelings, and is specific to particular situations. We are concerned here specifically with students' beliefs about their ability to understand and perform well in psychology. This may be independent of more general academic self-efficacy. Schunk (1991) has suggested four sources of information that we draw upon in order to arrive at our academic self-efficacy.

- Previous experience: students who have previously succeeded in tasks will generally tend to have higher self-efficacy for related tasks. Thus the psychology student who performs well in a modular exam will be confident of doing so again.
- Direct persuasion: feedback to students – formal and informal – can affect their perceptions of their ability to perform tasks.
- Observational learning: we tend to pick up on the self-efficacy of our peers. Where students are generally doing well individuals pick up on this and judge their own ability to succeed accordingly.
- Physiological cues: we constantly experience our physiological state and use this as a source of information about our current emotional state. If students feel anxious while performing a task they may judge their ability to perform that task as poor.

According to Bandura and his colleagues, the motivation to invest effort and persevere with a task is largely dependent on our beliefs about our competence in that task at that moment. Snowman and Biehler (2000) suggest three reasons for this. First, those with high levels of self-efficacy tend to choose more ambitious goals than those with lower levels. They may for example set out to master a task rather than merely to attain a minimum acceptable grade. Second, students with high levels of self-efficacy tend to expect more positive outcomes from a task and therefore see fit to invest more effort in attaining them. Finally, people with high self-efficacy tend to be less discouraged by occasional failure because they tend to attribute such failure to insufficient effort rather than lack of ability.

Improving student self-efficacy

There are a number of ways in which psychology teachers can improve the self-efficacy of their students. The general messages given out by teachers in the form of praise and recognition of achievement can help self-efficacy. There are however more targeted approaches. One such approach involves *goal* or *target* setting. When learners have concrete, realistic short-term goals to work towards, they can judge their self-efficacy in relation to these. There is clear evidence that, when used appropriately, setting goals or targets can enhance performance (see Jarvis, 2005 for a review). Highly explicit outcomes are preferable as they provide solid criteria against which individuals can judge their own achievements. Short-term goals are preferable as they are well remembered at the point where outcome is assessed.

Given the importance of observational learning in self-efficacy beliefs, another avenue to enhancing self-efficacy involves exposing learners to peer success. Nauseating as the phrase 'culture of achievement' can be when used by politicians, it is nonetheless quite true that developing such a classroom culture can enhance individuals' self-efficacy. The development of a culture of achievement can be attained by using sequences of carefully thought-out assessments that are manageable and link closely to recently covered syllabus content. One controversial strategy is to provide false positive feedback. Although empirically validated, this technique raises ethical issues as it means to some extent deceiving students. Perhaps a better approach is to focus heavily on skills development and link this to assessment. For example, thinking skills toolkits (see page 72) can be used to prepare students for AO2 assessments. This will allow very high levels of genuine success in the assessment.

Attributions of success and failure

Attribution is the cognitive process whereby we explain the causes of events. Bernard Weiner (1992) has developed a theory of attribution that has been particularly useful in understanding student motivation. Weiner points out that every time students succeed or fail at a task they attribute this success or failure to a cause. The technical term for this process is *causal inference*. Often we do not have sufficient information to make completely logical causal inferences, but instead rely on general beliefs about the situation and ourselves. These are called *causal schemata*.

Our attributions of success and failure can have a profound effect on motivation to tackle future tasks. Weiner identified three dimensions to the nature of attributions made by learners regarding success and failure. The first dimension is locus of control. *Locus of control* refers to the extent to which individuals believe they can control events. Generally, an internal locus of control is more adaptive than an external locus – if we believe we can alter events we tend to be more motivated to tackle them positively.

The second dimension to causality is *stability*. Causes of success and failure may be stable, i.e. they remain constant across situations (e.g. effort, task difficulty), or they may be unstable, i.e. they change from one situation to another (e.g. luck, mood). The final dimension is *controllability*. Table 7.2 shows a matrix of causal attributions resulting from combinations of controllability, locus of control and stability.

Table 7.2 **Factors affecting causal attributions of success and failure**

	Internal locus of control		External locus of control	
Controllability	Stable	Unstable	Stable	Unstable
Controllable	Typical effort	Atypical effort	Teacher bias	Atypical help
Uncontrollable	Ability	Mood	Task difficulty	Luck

Students with an internal locus of control tend to attribute results to their own actions and characteristics. Where results are judged to be controllable they are attributed to effort. When they are judged to be uncontrollable then ability and mood become the focus of causal inference. On the other hand, the student characterised by an external locus of control tends to attribute their successes and failures to features of the situation. Stable external causes include task difficulty (uncontrollable) and teacher bias (controllable). Unstable causes include luck and unusual help. Table 7.3 shows a range of students' responses to success and failure (adapted from Craske, 1988).

This range of responses can be explained in terms of Weiner's theory. For example good and bad 'luck' are external influences, therefore more likely to be attributions made by those with an external locus of control. Luck is also unstable and uncontrollable in nature. If we believe that luck is the primary factor affecting our success or failure we will probably not be motivated to make more effort on future occasions. An attribution of 'I am clever' is somewhat more motivating, being internal rather than external. However, it is also uncontrollable, and where we see results as being beyond our control there is limited motivation to make greater effort. According to Weiner the most adaptive type of causal inferences involve effort; when we attribute success and failure to the degree of effort committed to the task we should be maximally motivated to make great effort on future occasions.

Table 7.3 **Examples of causal inferences about success and failure**

Success	Failure
'I had good luck'	'I had bad luck'
'It was easy'	'It was too hard'
'I tried hard'	'I didn't try hard enough'
'I am clever'	'I'm not clever enough'

Working with student attributions

Attribution theory has a number of important implications for classroom practice. If psychology teachers can identify students who make unhelpful attributions of their successes and failures and work with them to alter these to more positive attributions they should in principle be able to improve their motivation. This can be formalised as a branch of cognitive behavioural therapy known as *attributional therapy* or be carried out more informally in everyday interaction with learners. Examples of the focus that work on attribution might take are shown in Box 7.5.

Box 7.5

Examples of alterations in learner attributions

- Uncontrollable → controllable attributions   e.g.   ability → effort.
- External → internal attributions   e.g.   luck → effort.
- Stable → unstable attributions   e.g.   potential → mood

Occasions arise frequently in the classroom when learners make comments like 'it was easy' in response to success or 'I'm just not up to this' in response to failure. It can be very helpful to challenge these attributions, suggesting for example that in fact a task was not easy, but that the student had in fact put in considerable effort and perhaps demonstrated a talent. This is an example of differentiation by response. Weiner's theory gives us a good basis for understanding how and when to make such challenges. As with all therapeutic techniques, however, a degree of caution is needed, and it is important that teachers do not throw out their experience and common sense and embrace techniques like attribution too religiously. The principle underlying all cognitive techniques is that the current beliefs are in some way incorrect. It is thus helpful for learners to attribute failure to lack of effort *provided they did not actually make sufficient effort*. However it is quite possible for students to make considerable effort and to fall foul of bad luck in exam questions or poor marking, and nothing could be more demotivating than to be told it was a result of lack of effort (Marshall, 1990). In such cases it may be more helpful to agree that the learner was unlucky and focus on the likelihood that next time they will probably have better luck.

Gender

At post-16 level female students in general achieve marginally better grades than males. This disparity is much greater in psychology than in most subjects. Table 7.4 shows the gendered 2005 A-level grade distribution of psychology (all boards combined) in comparison with grades across all subjects.

Whilst the gender disparity across all subjects is modest (A–C 66.7 male, 72.6 female; A–E male 95.4, female 97%), it is considerably greater in psychology, with A–C achievement in males being only 33.3% as opposed to 52.6% for females. For many psychologists gender is synonymous with feminism (Nicolson, 1997), and when we discuss gender differences we are almost always focusing on the ways in which women are disadvantaged. Whilst feminist commentators are quite correct to point out that in the past when male achievement outstripped female nobody identified a crisis (Francis and Skelton, 2001), teachers have a responsibility for all students and thus we find ourselves in the unusual position of trying to enhance the experience of males relative to that of females. Although this may make us uncomfortable, there is essentially no conflict between saying on the one hand that much traditional psychology marginalises the characteristics, needs and experiences of women, and on the other that currently male students underachieve relative to female students. These are separate issues and each can be addressed without diminishing the importance of the other.*

So why do boys underachieve? Younger *et al.* (2005) have identified the following possible factors:

- Neurological differences between male and female brains leading to different patterns of information processing.
- Cultural norms of masculinity that involve disregard for achievement and authority.
- Lower aspirations among male students.
- Greater maturity and social skills, and better learning strategies in female students.
- Different quality of interactions of male and female students with peers and teachers.

Table 7.4 **Comparison of disparities in A-level grades between males and females (%).**

		A	B	C	D	E	U
Psychology	Male	11.0	18.9	24.0	22.2	16.2	7.7
	Female	20.1	24.0	23.7	17.9	9.9	4.4
All subjects	Male	21.5	22.3	22.9	18.2	10.5	4.6
	Female	23.9	25.1	23.6	16.4	8.0	3.0

Source: *Guardian Education*

---

* Sexism in psychology is not within the scope of this chapter. See the 1997 special issue of *Psychology Teaching* for further information.

They suggest that tackling these generic problems requires intervention on four levels:

- Pedagogic: classroom-based approaches centred on teaching and learning.
- Individual: effective use of target-setting and mentoring.
- Organisational: ways of organising learning at the whole-school level.
- Socio-cultural: approaches that attempt to create an environment for learning where key boys and girls feel able to work with the aims and aspirations of the institution.

Subject-specific factors: is psychology a feminine subject?

Not to discount the potential importance of generic factors affecting male achievement, but given that gender differences in achievement are greater in psychology than in most subjects we should also consider the possibility that subject-specific factors are at work. One angle into this is to consider the differential achievement in different school subjects at Secondary level. Boys do well in maths and science, less so in arts subjects. If psychology as taught at post-16 level were actually as scientific and mathematical as it is often represented we might suppose that boys would have the advantage rather than girls. Clearly this is not the case.

Based on this we might cautiously propose that emphasising the 'hard science' and statistical aspects of psychology may advantage boys. Note that currently this is not empirically validated but represents a logical strategy. There may for example be parts of the psychology curriculum that are seen as traditionally feminine that can be enhanced for boys by inserting some hard science. For example primary caregiver-infant attachment and day care may be to some extent masculinised by emphasising methodological analysis of some key studies and by making reference to contemporary neuroscience, which has examined the effect of privation on brain development.

Topic options may provide another opportunity to cater for masculine interests. Specifications with applied options such as sport and criminal psychology make this more straightforward. Examples and resources offered to students may also be differentially appealing to boys and girls. Take for example social learning. Where this fits into the curriculum varies according to what specification is being followed, but social learning is often framed as a way of explaining children's developing behaviour – a 'feminine' area of psychology. By introducing the current debates about the effects of modelled aggression in televised football this can be made equally relevant to both genders.

Summary and conclusions

It is important to be clear that, in the classroom of the 21st century, differentiation does not simply mean having different resources, graded by difficulty to give to students of differing ability. Differentiation means having the resources, tasks, support systems and feedback that take account of the differing needs of individual students. As well as intelligence and academic ability (take care not to confuse these ideas), differentiation should take account of learning style and strategy. A word of caution is needed when talking about learning styles. Although learning styles certainly exist, they have numerous conceptual and practical problems, and we should be extremely cautious about some of the recommendations made by producers of commercial learning styles assessments packages. If we use a variety of teaching methods and make suggestions to individuals based on their individual strengths and weaknesses then we are differentiating by learning styles.

Students differ as well in terms of socio-cognitive variables including motivation and gender. It is possible to enhance motivation by boosting self-efficacy and by manipulating attributions of success and failure. Although it is well established that girls significantly outperform boys in psychology and despite the wealth of research into gender differences in general achievement, it remains unclear why boys are so disadvantaged in post-16 psychology. As well as the general types of strategy used to boost male achievement it may be possible to masculinise elements of the psychology curriculum.

One final word about differentiation. The word 'differentiation' often strikes terror into the hearts of teachers who fear that they are somehow meant to be providing tailor-made resources and activities for every student every lesson. Forget it! If you are producing user-friendly resources, making good use of ILT, making use of peer interaction, offering individualised feedback and using an appropriate range of examples in teaching then you are already differentiating. Relax.

Self-assessment questions

1. Suggest a modern definition of differentiation. How does this differ from more traditional definitions?

2. Discuss the relationship between ability, intelligence and achievement.

3. Is it worth keeping the concept of learning styles?

4. What is self-efficacy? How would you improve the self-efficacy of a psychology student?

5. Discuss gender differences in achievement in post-16 psychology.

Further reading

•••••• Francis, B. and Skelton, C. (2001) *Investigating Gender: Contemporary Perspectives in Education*. Open University Press, Buckingham.

•••••• Jarvis, M. (2005) *The Psychology of Effective Learning and Teaching*. Nelson Thornes, Cheltenham.

•••••• Riding, R. J. and Rayner, S. (1998) *Cognitive Styles and Learning Strategies*. David Fulton, London.

•••••• Younger, M., Warrington, M., Gray, J., Rudduck, J., McLellan, R., Bearne, E., Kershner, R. and Bricheno, P. (2005) *Raising Boys' Achievement*. DfES, London.

Appendix I

Publishers specialising in post-16 psychology

Causeway Press/Pearsons
Po Box 13
Ormskirk
L39 5HP
http://vig.pearsoned.co.uk/

Collins
77–85 Fulham Palace Road
London
W6 8JB
http://www.collins.co.uk/

Heinemann Educational
FREEPOST (OF1771)
PO Box 381
Oxford
OX2 8BR
http://www.heinemann.co.uk/

Hodder Headline
338 Euston Road
London
NW1 3BH
http://www.hodderheadline.co.uk/
index.asp?area=ed

Nelson Thornes Ltd
Delta Place
27 Bath Road
Cheltenham
Glos
GL53 7TH
http://www.nelsonthornes.com/

Oxford University Press
Great Clarendon Street
Oxford
OX2 7TW
http://www.oup.co.uk/oxed/secondary/

Palgrave Macmillan
Houndmills
Basingstoke
Hampshire
RG21 6XS
http://www.palgrave.com

Philip Allan Updates
Market Place
Deddington
Oxon
OX15 0SE
http://www.philipallan.co.uk/

Psychology Press
27 Church Road
Hove
East Sussex
BN3 2FA
http://www.psypress.co.uk

Appendix II

Professional bodies that support psychology teaching

The Association for the Study of Animal Behaviour (ASAB)
141 Newmarket Road
Cambridge
CB5 8HA
http://asab.nottingham.ac.uk/

The Association for the Teaching of Psychology (ATP)
c/o The British Psychological Society
St Andrews House
48 Princess Road East
Leicester
LE1 7DR
http://theatp.org/

The British Psychological Society (BPS)
St Andrews House
48 Princess Road East
Leicester
LE1 7DR
http://www.bps.org.uk/

The European Federation of Psychology Teaching Associations (EFPTA)
http://www.efpta.org

The National Institute on the Teaching of Psychology (NITOP)
2303 Naples Court
Champaign
IL 61822
USA
http://www.nitop.org/

The Society for the Teaching of Psychology (STP)
Le Moyne College
Syracuse
NY 13214
USA
http://teachpsych.lemoyne.edu/teachpsych/div/divindex.html

Teachers of Psychology in Secondary Schools (TOPSS)
Education Directorate
750 First Street, NE
Washington
DC 20002–4242
USA
http://www.apa.org/ed/topss/homepage.html

Appendix III

Journals specialising in the teaching of psychology

Essays from e-xcellence in Teaching
Produced by the Society for the Teaching of Psychology
Available free on-line
http://teachpsych.lemoyne.edu/teachpsych/eit/index.html

Psychology Learning & Teaching
Produced by the Higher Education Academy
Available free on-line
http://www.psychology.heacademy.ac.uk/html/plat_journal.asp

Psychology Teacher Network
Produced by TOPSS
Current issue free on-line
http://www.apa.org/ed/topss/homepage.html

Psychology Teaching
Produced by the Association for the Teaching of Psychology
Free to members

Psychology Teaching Review
Produced by the British Psychological Society Division for Teachers and
Researchers in Psychology
Free to members

Teaching of Psychology
Produced by the Society for the Teaching of Psychology
Free to members

Appendix IV

Awarding bodies offering post-16 psychology qualifications

AQA
GCSE, A-level, Access to HE, AEA
Stag Hill House
Guildford
Surrey
GU2 7XJ
http://www.aqa.org.uk/

Edexcel
A-level
190 High Holborn
London
WC1V 7BH
http://www.edexcel.org.uk/home/

International Baccalaureate
IB Diploma
Johannesgatan 20
Stockholm
SE-11138
Sweden
http://www.internationalbaccalaureate.co.uk/

NOCN
Access to HE
9 St James Court
Friar Gate
Derby
DE1 1BT
http://www.nocn.org.uk/

OCR
GCSE, A-level
Westwood Business Park
Westwood Way
Coventry
CV4 8JQ
http://www.ocr.org.uk/

SQA
Scottish Higher
24 Douglas Street
Glasgow
G2 7NQ
http://www.sqa.org.uk

References

Alloway, T., Wilson, G., Graham, J., and Krames, L. (2000) *Sniffy the Virtual Rat – Lite Version*. Thomson Learning, Berlmont.

Allport, D. A. (1980) Attention and Performance. In: *Cognitive Psychology: New Directions* (ed. Claxton, G.). Routledge, London.

Anderson, A., Howe, C., Soden, R., Halliday, J. and Low, J. (2001) Peer interaction and the learning of critical thinking in Further Education students. *Instructional Science*, **29**, 1–32.

Ausubel, D. P. (1968) *Educational Psychology: A Cognitive View*. Holt, New York.

Balch, W. R. (2005) Elaborations of introductory psychology terms: effects on test performance and subjective ratings. *Teaching of Psychology*, **32**, 29–33.

Bandura, A. (1986) *Social Foundations of Thought and Action*. Prentice Hall, Englewood Cliffs NJ.

Bandura, M. and Dweck, C. S. (1981) The relationship of conceptions of intelligence and achievement goals to achievement-related cognition, affect and behaviour. Unpublished manuscript, Harvard University.

Banister, P. (2003) Impact of post-16 qualifications on the undergraduate curriculum: views from heads of psychology departments. In: *Post-16 Qualifications in Psychology* (ed. McGuinness, C.). British Psychological Society, Leicester.

Barkham, M. and Mellor-Clark, J. (2000) Rigour and relevance: the role of practice-based evidence in the psychological therapies. In: *Evidence-based Counselling and Psychological Therapies* (eds. Rowland, N. and Goss, S.). Routledge, London.

BECTA (2003) *ICT Research*. http://www.becta.org.uk/research

Blair-Broeker, C. (2002) Bringing psychology to life. *Essays From e-xcellence in Teaching* 2, n.p.

Bloom, B. S. (ed.) (1956) *Taxonomy of Educational Objectives: The Classification of Educational Goals*, Handbook I, *Cognitive Domain*. McKay, New York.

Bolam, P. (2004) A case study on the development and use of an e-learning initiative. *Psychology Teaching*, Summer, 39–45.

Bowman, L. L. and Waite, B. M. (2003) Volunteering in research: student satisfaction and educational benefits. *Teaching of Psychology*, **30**, 102–106.

British Psychological Society (1997) *The Division for Teachers and Researchers in Psychology: About Us*. http://www.bps.org.uk/sub-sites$/dtrp/about.cfm

Bruntlett, S. (2001) Making and using multimedia: a critical examination of the learning opportunities. In: *Issues in Teaching Using ICT* (ed. Leask, M.). RoutledgeFalmer: London.

Burden, B. (1993) Psychology and cinema. In: *Teaching Psychology: Information and Resources* (eds. Rose, D and Radford, J.). British Psychological Society, Leicester.

Burns, A. (1998) Pop psychology or Ken behaving badly. *The Psychologist*, **11**, 7, 360.

Carlsmith, K. M. and Cooper, J. (2002) A persuasive example of collaborative learning. *Teaching of Psychology*, **29**, 132–135.

Churach, D. and Fisher, D. (2001) Science students surf the web: effects on constructivist classroom environments. *Journal of Computers in Mathematics and Science Teaching*, **20**, 221–247.

Clarke, C. (2004) Secretary of State for Education. http://www.becta.org.uk/corporate/index.cfm

Coffield, F., Moseley, D., Hall, E. and Ecclestone, K. (2004) *Should we be using learning styles? What research has to say to practice*. Learning and Skills Development Agency. https://www.lsda.org.uk/cims/order.aspx?code=041540&src=XOWEB

Cook, J. L. (2005) Constructing knowledge: the value of teaching from multiple perspectives. Paper delivered at the National Institute on the Teaching of Psychology (NITOP) annual conference.

Craik, F. I. M. and Lockhart, R. S. (1972) Levels of processing: a framework for memory research. *Journal of Verbal Learning and Verbal Behaviour*, **11**, 671–684.

Craske, M. L. (1988) Learned helplessness, self-worth motivation and attribution retraining for primary school children. *British Journal of Educational Psychology*, **58**, 152–164.

Dahlgreen, M. and Dahlgreen, L. (2002) Portraits of PBL: students' experiences of the characteristics of PBL in physiotherapy, computer engineering and psychology. *Instructional Science*, **30**, 111–127.

Daniel, D. B. (2005) Using PowerPoint to ruin a perfectly good lecture. Paper presented to the 1st Biennial Society for Research in Child Development (SCRD) Teaching of Developmental Science Institute, August.

Dickson, K. L., Miller, M. D. and Devoley, M. S. (2005) Effect of textbook study guides on student performance in introductory psychology. *Teaching of Psychology*, **32**, 34–39.

Diseth, A. (2002) The relationship between intelligence, learning styles, approaches to learning and academic achievement. *Scandinavian Journal of Educational Research*, **46,** 219–230.

Dunn, J. and Munn, P. (1985) Becoming a family member: family conflict and the development of social understanding in the first year. *Child Development*, **50**, 306–318.

Dweck, C. S. (2000) *Self-theories: Their Role in Motivation, Personality and Development*. Psychology Press, Philadelphia PA.

Dweck, C. S., Chiu, C. and Hong, Y. (1995) Implicit theories and their role in judgments and reactions: a world from two perspectives. *Psychological Inquiry*, **6**, 267–285.

Entwistle, N. J., Hounsell, D., Macaulay, C., Situnayke, G. and Tait, H. (1989) The Performance of Electrical Engineering Students in Scottish Higher Education. Final report to the Scottish Education Department. University of Edinburgh, Edinburgh.

Facione, P. A. and Facione, N. C. (1994) *Holistic Critical Thinking Scoring Rubric*. California Academic Press, Milbrae.

Facione, P. A. (1990) *Critical Thinking: A Statement of Expert Consensus for Purposes of Education Assessment and Instruction*. California Academic Press, Milbrae.

Facione, P. A. (1995) The California Critical Thinking Skills Test. http://www.insightassessment.com

Falchikov, N. and Goldfinch, J. (2000) Student peer assessment in Higher Education: a meta-analysis comparing peer and teacher marks. *Review of Educational Research*, **70**, 287–322.

Faria, L. (1998) Personal conceptions of intelligence, attributions and school achievement: development of a comprehensive model of inter-relations during adolescence. *Psicologia: Revista da Associacao Psicologia*, **12**, 101–113.

Faria, L. and Fontaine, A. M. (1997) Adolescents' person conceptions of intelligence: the development of a new scale and some exploratory evidence. *European Journal of Psychology of Education*, **12**, 51–62.

Felder, R. M. and Silverman, L. K. (1988) Learning and teaching styles in engineering education. *Engineering Education*, **78**, 674–681.

Fisher, R. (1995) *Teaching Children to Think*. Nelson Thornes, Cheltenham.

Fitz-Gibbon, C. T. and Vincent, L. (1994) *Candidates' Performance in Science and Mathematics at A-level*. School Curriculum and Assessment Authority (SCAA), London.

Flavell, J. H. (1985) *Cognitive Development*. Prentice Hall, Englewood Cliffs NJ.

Francis, B. and Skelton, C. (2001) *Investigating Gender: Contemporary Perspectives in Education*. Open University Press, Buckingham.

Gage, N. L. and Berliner, D. C. (1991) *Educational Psychology*. Houghton Mifflin, Boston.

Gorenflo, D. W. and McConnell, J. V. (1991) The most frequently cited journal articles and authors in introductory psychology textbooks. *Teaching of Psychology*, **18**, 8–12.

Grant, F. (2004) Free statistics software: yours, free to keep. *Scientific Computing*, October, n.p.

Green, R. J. (2005) Teaching psychology through film, video. American Psychological Society. http://www.psychologicalscience.org/teaching/tips/tips_0703.cfm

Gregorc, A. F. (1979) Learning/teaching styles: Potent forces behind them. *Educational Leadership* **36**, 234–236.

Griggs, R. A. and Marek, P. (2001) Similarity of introductory psychology textbooks: reality or illusion. *Teaching of Psychology*, **28**, 254–256.

Grigorenko, E. L., Jarvin, L. and Sternberg, R. J. (2002) School-based tests of the triarchic theory of intelligence: three settings, three samples, three syllabi. *Contemporary Educational Psychology*, **27**, 167–208.

Gurung, R. A. R. (2003) Pedagogical aids and student performance. *Teaching of Psychology*, **30**, 92–95.

Gurung, R. A. R. (2004) Pedagogical aids: learning enhancers or dangerous detours? *Teaching of Psychology*, **31**, 164–6.

Hargreaves, D. H. (1996) *Teaching as a research-based profession: possibilities and prospects*. Teacher Training Authority (TTA) annual lecture.

Hay McBer (2000*) Research Into Teacher Effectiveness*. Department for Education and Employment (DfES), London.

Hayes, N. (1998) Can teaching psychology transform popular culture? *Psychology Teaching Review*, **7**, 44–54.

Hillage, J., Pearson, R., Anderson, A. and Tamkin, P. (1998) *Excellence in Research in Schools*. Her Majesty's Stationery Office (HMSO), London.

Hirschler, S. and Banyard, P. (2003) Post-16 students: views and experiences of studying psychology. In: *Post-16 Qualifications in Psychology* (ed. McGuinness, C.). British Psychological Society, Leicester.

Howarth, G. (1997) *Using ATP software to teach psychology*. Proceedings of the 15th Association for the Teaching of Psychology (ATP) Conference. University of Surrey, July, 126–128.

Howitt, D. and Owusu-Bempah, K. (1994) *The Racism of Psychology: Time for Change*. Harvester Wheatsheaf, Hemel Hempstead.

Jackson, S. L., Griggs, R. A., Koenig, C. S., Christopher, A. N. and Marek, P. (2000*) A Compendium of Introductory Psychology Texts: 1997–2000*. Office of Teaching Resources in Psychology (OTRP), Galveston TX.

Jarvis, M. (2000) Teaching psychodynamic psychology: from discourse analysis towards a model of reflective practice. *Psychology Teaching*, **8**, 13–21.

Jarvis, M. (2001) *Angles on Child Psychology*. Nelson Thornes, Cheltenham.

Jarvis, M. (2003) Survey of psychology teachers' views on continual professional development. In: *Post-16 Qualifications in Psychology* (ed. McGuinness, C.). British Psychological Society, Leicester.

Jarvis, M. (2004) The rigour and appeal of psychology A-level. *Education Today*, **54**, 24–28.

Jarvis, M. (2005) *The Psychology of Effective Learning and Teaching*. Nelson Thornes, Cheltenham.

Jarvis, M. (in press) A systematic review of free statistics software: what works for post-16 psychology? *Psychology Teaching*.

Jarvis, M., Russell, J. and Gorman, P. (2004*) Angles on Psychology*, 2nd edition. Nelson Thornes, Cheltenham.

Karau, S. J. and Williams, K. D. (1993) Social loafing: a meta-analytic review. *Journal of Personality and Social Psychology*, **65**, 681–706.

Kelly, G. A. (1955) *The Psychology of Personal Constructs*. Norton, New York.

Kerry, T. and Wilding, M. (2004) *Effective Classroom Teacher*. Longman, London.

Kimble, G. A. (1999) Functional behaviourism: a plan for the unity of psychology. Invited address presented at the annual meetings of the American Psychological Association, Boston.

Larkin, M. (2002) Using scaffolding instruction to optimize learning. *ERIC Digest*

Lavender, A., Thompson, L. and Burns, S. (2003) Training and staff retention: National issues and findings from the South Thames (Salomons) Clinical Psychology Training Scheme. *Clinical Psychology*, **21**, 20–26.

Leafe, D. (2001) Intranets: developing a learning community. In: *Issues in Teaching Using ICT* (ed. Leask, M.). RoutledgeFalmer, London.

Leeming, F. C. (2002) The exam-a-day procedure improves performance in psychology classes. *Teaching of Psychology*, **29**, 210–212.

Levy, S., Stroessner, S. and Dweck, C. (1998) Stereotype formation and endorsement: the role of implicit theories. *Journal of Personality and Social Psychology*, **74**, 1421–1436.

Linnell, M. (2003) Second year undergraduate psychology students: views on their study of post-16 psychology. In: *Post-16 Qualifications in Psychology* (ed. McGuinness, C.). British Psychological Society, Leicester.

Luiten, J., Ames, W. and Ackerman, G. (1980) A meta-analysis of the effects of advance organisers on learning and retention. *American Educational Research Journal*, **17**, 211–282.

McCune, V. and Entwistle, N. (2000) The deep approach to learning: analytic abstraction and idiosyncratic development. Paper presented at the Innovations in Higher Education Conference, Helsinki.

McGhee, P. (2001) *Thinking Psychologically*. Palgrave, Basingstoke.

McGuinness, C. (1999) *From Thinking Skills to Thinking Classrooms*. DfEE, London.

McGuinness, C. (ed.) (2003) *Post-16 Qualifications in Psychology*. British Psychological Society, Leicester.

Maki, R., Maki, W. S., Patterson, M. and Whittaker, P. D. (2000) Evaluation of a web-based introductory psychology course: 1. Learning and satisfaction in on-line versus lecture courses. *Behaviour Research Methods, Instruments and Computers*, **32**, 230–239.

Marek, P., Griggs, R. A. and Christopher, A. N. (1999) Pedagogical aids in textbooks: do college students' perceptions justify their prevalence? *Teaching of Psychology*, **26**, 11–19.

Marshall, S. P. (1990) What students learn and remember from word instruction. Paper presentation at the annual meeting of the American Educational Research Association, Boston.

Mayo, J. A. (2004) Repertory grid as a means to compare and contrast developmental theorists. *Teaching of Psychology*, **31**, 178–180.

Meyers, S. A. (1997) Increasing student participation and productivity in small-group activities for psychology classes. *Teaching of Psychology*, **24**, 105–115.

Moon, H. (2001) Psychology teachers shaping psychology. In: *Essays From Excellence in Teaching 2000–2001* (eds. Buskit, W., Hevern, V. and Hill, G. W.). Society for the Teaching of Psychology, Galveston TX.

Morris, P. (2003) Not the soft option. *The Psychologist*, **16**, 510–511.

Mottarella, K., Fritzche, B. and Parrish, T. (2005) Who learns more? Achievement scores following web-based versus classroom instruction in psychology courses. *Psychology Learning and Teaching*, **4**, 51–54.

National Learning Network (2004) Learning Technologies. http://www.ccm.ac.uk/ltech/ilt/default.asp

Nevid, J. S. and Lampmann, J. L. (2003) Effects on content acquisition of signalling key concepts in text material. *Teaching of Psychology*, **30**, 227–230.

Nicolson, P. (1997) Gender and psychology: adding gender to the curriculum. *Psychology Teaching*, **5**, 13–18.

Nisbett, J. and Shucksmith, J. (1986) *Learning Strategies*. Routledge and Kegan Paul, London.

Norton, L. (2004) *Psychology Applied Learning Scenarios (PALS): A Practical Introduction to Problem-based Learning Using Vignettes for Psychology Lecturers*. LTSN, York.

Nummedal, S. G., Benson, J. B. and Chew, S. L. (2002) Disciplinary styles in the scholarship of learning and teaching: a view from psychology. In: *Disciplinary Styles in the Scholarship of Learning and Teaching: Exploring Common Ground* (eds. Huber, M. T. and Morreale, S. P.). American Association for Higher Education, Washington DC.

Ocampo, C., Prieto, L. R., Whittlesey, V., Connor, J., Janco-Gidley, J., Mannix, S. and Sare, K. (2003) Diversity research in *Teaching of Psychology*: summary and recommendations. *Teaching of Psychology*, **30**, 5–18.

O'Hare, L. and McGuinness, C. (2004) Skills and attributes developed by psychology undergraduates: ratings by undergraduates, postgraduates, academic psychologists and professional practitioners. *Psychology Learning and Teaching*, **4**, 35–42.

Oley, N. (2002) Extra credit and peer tutoring: impact on the quality of writing in introductory psychology in an open admissions college. In: *Handbook for Teaching Introductory Psychology*, vol. 3 (ed. Griggs, R. A.). LEA, Mahwah NJ.

Palmer, S. (2003) Enquiry based learning can maximise a student's potential. *Psychology Learning and Teaching*, **2**, 82–86.

Papert, S. (1996) *The Connected Family: Bridging the Digital Generation Gap*. Longstreet Press, Atlanta GA.

Paul, R. (1993) *Critical Thinking: How to Prepare Students for a Rapidly Changing World*. Foundation for Critical Thinking, Rohnert Park CA.

Pennington, H. (2000) Can American introductory textbooks help us teach critical thinking about psychology? *Psychology Teaching*, **8**, 22–24.

Perkins, D. V. and Saris, R. N. (2001) A jigsaw classroom technique for undergraduate statistics courses. *Teaching of Psychology*, **28**, 111–113.

Perlman, B. and McCann, L. I. (1999) Developing teaching portfolios. Workshop presented at the Mid-America Conference for Teachers of Psychology, Evansville.

Pheiffer, G., Andrew, D., Green, M. and Holley, D. (2003) The role of learning styles in integrating and empowering learners. *Investigations in University Teaching and Learning*, **1**, 36–39.

QCA (2001) *Five-year review of standards: psychology A-level*. QCA, London.

Reynolds, M. (1997) Learning styles: a critique. *Management Learning*, **28**, 2, 115–133.

Riding, R. J. (1991) Cognitive Styles Analysis. Learning and Training Technology, Birmingham.

Riding, R. J. and Rayner, S. (1998) *Cognitive Styles and Learning Strategies*. David Fulton, London.

Rossi, M., Keeley, J. and Buskit, W. (2005) High school psychology and student performance in the college introductory psychology course. *Teaching of Psychology*, **32**, 52–54.

Rusico, J. (2001) Administering quizzes at random to increase students' reading. *Teaching of Psychology*, **28**, 204–206.

Rust, J. and Golombok, S. (1999) *Modern Psychometrics*. Routledge, London.

Sappington, J., Kinsey, K. and Munasayac, K. (2002) Two studies of reading compliance among college students. *Teaching of Psychology*, **29**, 272–274.

Schon, D. A. (1983) *The Reflective Professional: How Professionals Think in Action*. Avebury, Aldershot.

Schon, D. A. (1987) *Educating the Reflective Practitioner.* Jossey Bass Wiley, San Francisco CA.

Schunk, D. H. (1991) Self-efficacy and academic motivation. *Educational Psychologist,* **26**, 207–232.

Selinger, M. (2001) The role of the teacher: teacherless classrooms? In: *Issues in Teaching Using ICT* (ed. Leask, M.). RoutledgeFalmer, London.

Shapiro, D. (2002) Reviewing the scientist-practitioner model. *The Psychologist,* **15**, 232–234.

Sizer, T. R. (1992) *Horace's Compromise: The Dilemma of the American High School*. Houghton Mifflin, Boston.

Smith, S. M. and Woody, P. C. (2000) Interactive effect of multimedia instruction and learning styles. *Teaching of Psychology,* **27**, 220–223.

Snowman, J. and Biehler, R. (2000) *Psychology Applied to Teaching*. Houghton Mifflin, Boston.

Sternberg, R. J. (1997) What does it mean to be smart? *Educational Leadership,* **54**, 20–24.

Sternberg, R. J. (1999) A comparison of three models for teaching psychology. *Psychology Teaching Review,* **8**, 37–43.

Sternberg, R. J. and Clinkenbeard, P. R. (1995) A triarchic model for identifying, teaching and assessing gifted children. *Roeper Review,* **17**, 255–260.

Sternberg, R. J., Torff, B. and Grigorenko, E. L. (1998) Teaching triarchically improves school achievement. *Journal of Educational Psychology,* **00**, 1–11.

Sternberg, R. J. and Grigorenko, E. L. (1999) In praise of dilettantism. *APS Observer,* **12**, 37–38.

Sutton, P. (2000) Using lecture notes on the Internet as learning support materials for lectures: student and staff perspectives on note-taking. *Psychology Teaching Review,* **9**, 26–37.

Taggart, A. (2004) *ILT in Hampshire, England – Past, Present and Future. How Has ILT in Hampshire Developed and Can it be Improved for Future Learners?* Liverpool University.

Tharp, R. and Gallimore, R. (1991). A theory of teaching as assisted performance. In: *Learning to Think* (eds. Light, P., Sheidon, S. and Littleton, K.). Routledge, London.

Tombs, S. (2004) Writing, arguing and evaluation – the perspective from Higher Education. *Psychology Teaching,* Summer, 36–38.

Training Press Releases (2001) http://www.trainingpressreleases.com/newsstory.asp?NewsID=108.

Tufte, E. (2004) PowerPoint is evil. *Wired,* **9**, n.p.

Usher, R., Bryant, I. and Johnston, R. (1997) *Adult Education and the Postmodern Challenge: Learning Beyond the Limits*. Routledge, London.

Venneman, S. S. and Knowles, L. R. (2005) Sniffing out efficacy: Sniffy Lite, a virtual animal lab. *Teaching of Psychology,* **32**, 66–68.

Vidal-Abarca, E. and Sanjose, V. (1998) Levels of comprehension of scientific prose: the role of text variables. *Learning and Instruction,* **8**, 215–233.

Walker, K. (2004) Why do sixth form students choose psychology: a report of research in one institution. *Psychology Teaching,* Summer, 29–35.

Weiner, B. (1992) *Human Motivation: Metaphors, Theories and Research*. Sage, Thousand Oaks CA.

Wilkinson, J. D. and Campbell, E. A. (1997) *Psychology in Counselling and Therapeutic Practice*. Wiley, Chichester.

Williams, R. L., Oliver, R., Allin, J. L., Winn, B. and Booher, C. S. (2003) Psychological critical thinking as a course predictor and outcome variable. *Teaching of Psychology*, **30**, 220–223.

Wilson, V. (2000) *Educational Forum on Teaching Thinking Skills*. Scottish Executive Education Department, Edinburgh.

Witkin, H. A. (1964) Origins of cognitive style. In: *Cognition: Theory, Research, Promise* (ed. Scheerer, C.). Harper & Row, New York.

Youell, A. (2003) *Students Entering Higher Education Institutions With Access Qualifications 2002/3*. Higher Education Statistics Agency, Cheltenham.

Younger, M., Warrington, M., Gray, J., Rudduck, J., McLellan, R., Bearne, E., Kershner, R. and Bricheno, P. (2005) *Raising Boys' Achievement*. DfES, London.

Zechmeister, J. S. and Zechmeister, E. B. (2000) Introductory psychology textbooks and psychology's core concepts. *Teaching of Psychology*, **27**, 6–11.

Zeichner, K. and Tabachnick, B. (2001) Reflections on reflective teaching. In: *Teacher Development: Exploring Our Own Practice* (ed. Solar, J., Craft, A. and Burgess, H.). Paul Chapman, London.

Zinkiewicz, L., Hammond, N. and Trapp, A. (2003) *Applying Psychology Disciplinary Knowledge to Psychology Teaching and Learning*. LTSN, York.

Zinkiewicz, L. and Trapp, A. (2004) *Widening and Increasing Participation: Challenges and Opportunities for Psychology Departments*. LTSN, York.

Index

Page reference in italics indicate boxes or tables